SOUTH AMHERST

641.5 M
Mackie, Cristine
Life and food in the Caribbean.

SEP 2 8 1992

DATE DUE			
NOV 3 1992			
NOV 1 7 1992			
DEC 8 1992			
JAN 0 4 1993			
MAR 2 3 1993			
MAR 1 1 1994			
APR 2 7 1996			
MAR 1 8 1999			

201-9500   PRINTED IN U.S.A.

LIFE AND FOOD IN THE CARIBBEAN

LIFE AND FOOD
IN THE CARIBBEAN

CRISTINE MACKIE

NEW AMSTERDAM
New York

To Vicky Hayward

First published in the United States of America in 1992 by
NEW AMSTERDAM BOOKS
171 Madison Avenue
New York, NY 10016
by arrangement with George Weidenfeld and Nicolson Ltd., London.

Library of Congress Cataloging-in-Publication Data

MacKie, Cristine.
   Life and food in the Caribbean/Cristine MacKie.
      p. cm.
   Includes bibliographical references and indexes.
   ISBN 1-56131-029-8 (alk. paper)
    1. Cookery, Caribbean. 2. Caribbean Area—Social life and
customs. I. Title.
TX716.AlM23 1992
394.1'2'09729—dc20   91-35628
                                            CIP

Series Editor: Vicky Hayward
All illustrations by Liz Gibbons

This book is printed on acid-free paper.

Manufactured in the United States of America.
10 9 8 7 6 5 4 3 2 1

CONTENTS

rebellion on Constantine Sylvester's estate – the devoted hen – salting –
liver marinaded in lime juice – Cromwell's 'Western Design' – the sugar-
cane fields – kill-devil liquor and Grenada rumpot – the 'Barbadosed'
Irishmen

The Foremost Men in the World · 66

The enslaved African – Gustavus's memories – rice and peas – market day
– *metagee* – making coconut oil – caramelized meats – yams and plantain
– harvesting corn – *cou-cou* and *fou-fou* – life on Thistlewood's estate –
duckanoo – feasts and rituals – kingfish with chestnut sauce – lobster
callaloo – the local rumshop

Unseasoned Émigrés · 106

From Madeira to Trinidad – planting cocoa – the Mendes family – salt-
cod steaks in peppered olive oil – *piri piri* – sautéd conch – *festas* – hare in
white rum and allspice – chorizo and ackee salad – fearing the *soucouyant*
– limed melongene – the 'provisions merchants'

Mandarins and Rice Growers · 130

The coffee cultivators – recruiting the Chinese – noodles and chow mein –
memories of a restaurateur – the watercress beds – fish and watercress
soup – the oyster *marchands* – fried rice – pork in honey and soya sauce –
beef in five-spice – emancipation – Creole resentment

From East to West · 149

The indentured Indian – *chappatis* – castes and customs – accra and floats
– lobster fruit curry and massala fowl curry – the revolt of the women –
Yseult's diary – a Hindu wedding – sauces and pickles – festival dishes –
the breadnut

ACKNOWLEDGEMENTS

My thanks go firstly to my husband, who has been unfailingly patient as I probed again and again into his marvellous memory of his early life in the Caribbean. Then especially to Coralie Hepburn for all her good help; Mrs Chung-Steele of the Bird's Nest Restaurant, Grenada; and Mr Peter Mendes for giving me the first chapter from the manuscript by his father on the history of the Mendes family's journey from Madeira to Trinidad, 1846–1897. I also wish to acknowledge and thank the staff of the Bristol Archives, British Library, Department of History of the University of the West Indies, Grenadian Tourist Board, Institute of Jamaica, Jamaica High Commission, Public Records Office, Royal Commonwealth Society, Warwick University Caribbean Studies and West India Committee; Alan Davidson; Smokey Joe; and the many people in England and the West Indies who often unknowingly helped me by being prepared to spend time talking about their life and family, past and present.

COOK'S NOTES

CANE LIQUOR/BRANDY   A lightly flavoured rum or a fine brandy may be substituted, but it should, if possible, be of the best quality.

CARAMELIZING   For ½–1 kg (1–2 lbs) of meat, cover the bottom of your pan with 120 ml (4 floz) of oil and add 30–60 g (1–2 oz) of white sugar. Brown sugar does work, but you must stir to amalgamate the oil and sugar for much longer. As the mixture heats up, it will become a clear dark rich-mahogany colour. Stir well with a wooden spoon. Use gloves when putting in the meat and make sure it is absolutely dry and free of any seasoning. It may be necessary to remove the pan from the heat for a moment or two as you do this to prevent the caramel from becoming bitter. Return the pan to the heat, perhaps lowering it a little. Leave the meat to turn a rich golden brown and stir to coat it on all sides.

CHILLIES   These may be any of the following variety: bird pepper, Guinea pepper or African pepper. They are vital in Caribbean cooking and are used in a subtle way, not so much for heat but as a flavouring. In the North today you will mostly find bird peppers, which are small and extremely hot, or seasoning peppers, which can be hot or mild. The mild ones are delicious to eat in salads or simply fried or chopped up to season meat and fish. They have all the aroma of their more pungent relations, without the consequences. Use gloves when chopping and de-seeding them.

COCONUT CREAM   An alternative to grating the coconut meat would be to use ⅓ bar of coconut cream: Add to 200–600 ml (⅓–1 pint) of boiling water and stir until it is completely dissolved.

COCONUT MILK   This should be made fresh just before you need to use it. Chop the 'meat', or white flesh, into small pieces, then fill the blender with 600 ml (1 pint) of water. Slowly add the pieces of coconut flesh and blend until it has all broken down and has a grated appearance. Then pour the mixture through a strong cloth, collecting the milk as you squeeze in a large bowl beneath.

COCONUT OIL   This should be removed from the fridge at least two hours before use, since it can solidify and become white in appearance. In England I always keep it in a warm place to prevent this.

CURRY POWDER   I would not normally recommend any curry powder, for it is better to make your own. In the West Indies there are one or two packaged varieties, such as Chief or Chef, which are so good that everyone uses them and they do give certain dishes a standard characteristic flavour. Elsewhere I suggest that you use a very mild-flavoured one and add the heat with chillies.

LIMES   In the Caribbean these are so plentiful that there is no need to worry about making them last, but in England they can be expensive. If you wish to use just a part of it, cut out a segment cleanly without squeezing the fruit and the remainder will last for quite a while.

MEAT OR FISH STOCK   When the recipe suggests adding extra liquid, be it water, stock or wine, heat it thoroughly, without boiling it, before adding it to the dish. When changing climates it is easy to be heavy handed with the salt. To be safe use a teaspoon for 500 g (1 lb) of meat, 500 g (1 lb) of flour or 1 litre (1¾ pints) of stock. It is better to adjust afterwards if you need to.

ONIONS   When I refer to mild onions I recommend using Spanish.

SEASONING   or 'sisining'. This is a marvellous blend of limes, onions, garlic, coriander and spices. Meat and fish can be marinaded in it for a few hours or overnight to great effect, and it will keep in the fridge for months. Use a whole bunch of coriander leaves and stalks, 1 large onion, 6 spring onions (sives), 3–4 cloves of garlic, 3–5 cm (1–2 inches) of fresh peeled ginger, 1 tablespoon of black peppercorns, 1 teaspoon of salt, 2 tablespoons each of vegetable oil and malt or wine vinegar, 1–2 seasoning peppers and the juice of a small lime. Blend all the ingredients together.

TROPICAL FISH   If you buy tropical fish that has been frozen, be sure to ask if it was gutted before it was frozen as the flesh can easily be tainted. Now the fish is often flown in fresh and on ice, so that it may be frozen successfully – but again gut it first.

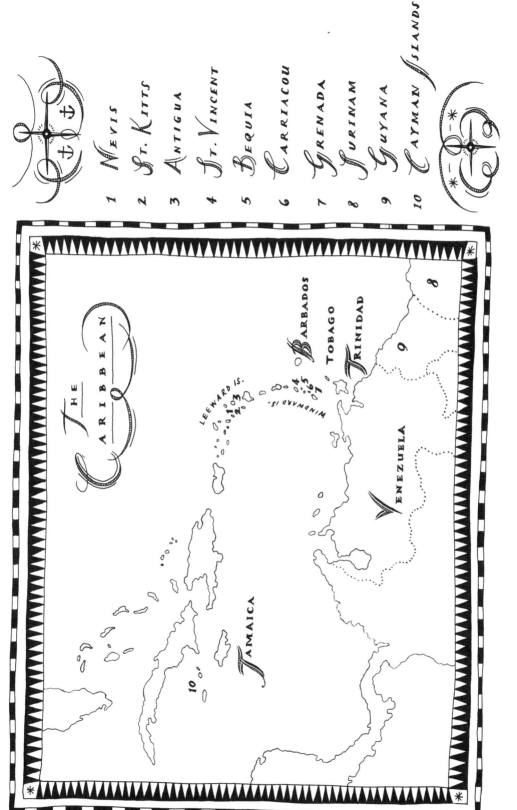

THE CARIBBEAN

1 NEVIS
2 ST. KITTS
3 ANTIGUA
4 ST. VINCENT
5 BEQUIA
6 CARRIACOU
7 GRENADA
8 SURINAM
9 GUYANA
10 CAYMAN ISLANDS

LEEWARD IS.
WINDWARD IS.
BARBADOS
TOBAGO
TRINIDAD
VENEZUELA
JAMAICA

INTRODUCTION

*What was the Caribbean? A green pond mantling
behind the Great House columns of Whitehall,
behind the Greek facades of Washington*

Derek Walcott

From 10° north of the equator to the tropic of Cancer lie the islands of
the Caribbean, scattered from Trinidad in the south, close to the South
American coast, to Jamaica and Cuba in the north-west, just under the
tip of America's Florida Cays.

Since the fifteenth century, when Europe first braved the Atlantic
crossing to the New World and the Pope instructed, 'Attack, subject
and reduce to perpetual slavery the Saracens, pagans and other
enemies of Christ,' travellers to the Caribbean have been writing,
mostly in ravishing terms, of what they found there. Clearly they were
as moved and sometimes as awe-inspired as I have been generations
later.

The countries of the north still know only the stereotyped images – white beaches, crystal clear seas and palm trees – which linger long in the mind. But the Caribbean is indeed an aesthetic in its own right, as full of emotion as a work of art. One is often overwhelmed by the freshness of the air, the light that fills you and the ground that provides for you. Viewed by day from the sea, many of the islands still appear untouched, the quintessence of the modern idea of a tropical pictorial poem, often fecund with vegetation and bird life. Some are fringed by a narrow strand of coral, lapped by shallow opal waters. Others rise sheer and stark, their black volcanic beaches glittering in the heat.

At dusk the islands lie like grey prehistoric creatures, seemingly slumbering, their ancient backbones rising from the sea to varying heights from which a multitude of rivers and streams cascade down to the coast, engraving their progress over the millions of years since the islands were first spewed forth in hideous convulsions of volcanic upheaval. It is hardly surprising that this part of the world has provoked such a deep sense of romance and fantasy in travellers.

For the indigenous people, however, the Caribbean is mostly a place to look out from. Their story is one of successive groups of conquerors and conquered, which began almost exactly 500 years ago when Columbus discovered the islands. It is an absorbing and extraordinary historical tale, and it is the subject of this book.

The tale has not always been an easy one to unravel. The tropics devour the past, leaving one obliged to return to the north where archives have remained, often in private collections for many generations, before giving up their secrets. Here can be found some evidence that testifies to the efforts made by the European colonizers through the centuries. They have also left their traces in stone forts standing on bluffs and promontories as grey reminders of past struggles to hold on to the islands. Their magnificently proportioned great houses – now crumbling under the rapacious greed of the tropical vines – and the smaller wooden estate houses are always beautifully placed on some high hilltop overlooking the sugar factory below, with trade winds cooling the freshly painted shingles.

But what of the people who were enslaved and indentured from around the world? Their cry has gone almost unheard. Who were these people who came from Africa, Asia and Europe, who worked with such stamina and resourcefulness on the sugar plantations? What remains of those poor souls? Their mystery, it seems to me, has penetrated deeply into the stonework of the old ruined estates and the surrounding lands, where you may still find vestiges of the old morasses, trenches and canals. In these places I am flooded by a connection with I know not what, and an overwhelming feeling of a past that is missing. Conrad wrote in *Heart of Darkness* of the meaning of an episode. He explained that it was not inside like a kernel, but outside, enveloping the tale which brought it out, only as a glow brings out a haze, in the likeness of one of those misty halos that are sometimes made visible by the spectral illumination of moonshine. And so, in the various episodes of the Caribbean's past, we are left to find our own illuminations.

It was through the West Indian kitchen in Barbados, Jamaica, Trinidad and all the other British islands of the Caribbean, that I began to find out about the people who came to work and settle in the islands. Because of the benign climatic conditions of the islands, blessed with some of the richest soils in the world, the different peoples who have settled here developed a hybrid cuisine with many fascinating strands. Here is to be found a blend of flavours and styles which helps to tell the story of those who left little else behind them. In it can be found the myriad ethnic strains of Caribbean voices.

Since my research began, a considerable amount of information from diaries, letters and household accounts, written by the people who chronicled their daily lives in the West Indies since the 1600s, has become available. The fresh light shed by this new material has enabled me to discover an altogether different picture of their lives from the often false one painted by visitors in the past, which tended to support a short-sighted government policy at home.

It was in the early sixteenth century, when the scent of the tobacco leaf was in the air, that this stratified cultural history began. Charles II was advised that it was unwise and unprofitable to allow the Spanish and Dutch to be absolute lords of these parts. The first British to arrive on the island of Barbados met with the Amerindians and learnt much from them about planting in the tropics and how to survive and feed themselves. Through the years that followed, the British way of cooking remained a constant framework in the background, which all subsequent groups drew from or contributed to.

A century later came the realization that there was great profit to be made in planting sugar-cane in this sweet spot of earth. It became an irresistible magnet, drawing colonists and workers from around the world to build up the great sugar estates. First came servants from England – freemen, debtors, and the like from Newgate Gaol, then defeated political rebels – and later came the enslaved Africans, indentured Portuguese, Chinese and Indians. Each, in turn, brought their traditional foodstuffs and cooking techniques which, over the centuries, have been woven into a vibrant and distinctive cuisine.

I was born at a time when air fares to the Caribbean have been reasonable enough to enable me to go many times during the last twenty years, even living there for months at a time; and it was natural, as an English person, that I should go to the British Caribbean islands as opposed to the Spanish, French or Dutch islands. When I was at the stage of simply absorbing such extraordinary new experiences, I was hardly aware of the Englishness of it all. But soon, travelling between the islands, I met with all the different groups through my own work or from my passion to see inside their kitchens. I realized that, although they might be from Africa, India or Portugal, they all had something in common in the way they spoke and prepared their food. Their apparent lack of a past seemed more and more strange, for it must have been as rich as ours, but all had adopted that very Englishness that still pervades life in the once British West Indian islands. I returned to England where it all began. I am really as fascinated by the story of the men and women of England who began it all – many of whom sailed to the West Indies from ports such as Lyme Regis, Weymouth and Plymouth in my beloved West Country – as in the peoples who followed from around the world to join their empire.

THE SHELLFISH GATHERERS

*There were still shards of an ancient pastoral
in those shires of the island where the cattle drank
their pools of shadow from an older sky.*

Derek Walcott

Under the tropical canopy, where the sun turns on reaching its greatest declination north or south, the islands of the West Indies lie basking in the cyan-tinted shallows. They form no more than a dotted line, often only a few miles in breadth and width, over a distance of some 1,500 miles between the seas of the Caribbean and Atlantic.

Much has been said about the beauty of this part of the world, but the words seldom convey the complete feeling of being at one with the elements inspired by the most unspoilt islands. One's feet are on terra firma, but the eye and ear are made consummate by the circular world above and below, of sometimes overpoweringly contradictory forces. The sea and sky encircle one from horizon to horizon. Above, are unceasing winds and swirling clouds, intermittently burgeoning heavenward in billowing white explosions; below, ferreous clouds race in from the far horizon bringing squalls which threaten the seas and whip up the spray in a roar across the reef. As fast as they come, they sweep off again, taking with them the violent sea. Small drops of the purest water are left clinging to the bougainvillea leaves, scoured fresh and glistening green in the new sun. The crimson blossoms are undiminished by the sun's saturating rays and through the fresh cut-glass air, tinged with a deep reddish-blue hue from the rain-washed blossoms, the seas again offer up their lagoon-like tranquillity. Within the reef, the depths are revealed by beautiful streaks of alternating violet, blues and greens, and by the iridescent spray and roar of the waters still on the reef.

Where the reefs are still intact, the fish life is marvellously abundant and translucent. In the cerulean water, arthropodal bodies such as the lobsters, prawns and shrimps bask easily and confidently in the sun-warmed shallows. Because the ocean floor of the Caribbean sea is made up of innumerable shattered particles of coral, nothing can move unnoticed against this often blindingly white backcloth, and hand or spear fishing is made all the easier. But it is also hazardous in the extreme. The sea floor is rich in sea eggs, with black sharp spines up to 30 cm long. If you tread on them unawares, the end breaks off into the flesh, practically paralysing you with pain.

The dark glossy green foliage of the manchineel tree bends low over the narrow bleached-white shore, enticing you into its poisonous shade; its fruit, like smooth green limes, bob in the shallows and scent the salted air with their peachy perfume. It is a tropical tree of the spurge family; scourge would be more appropriate since if the skin brushes against the leaves or fruit, it is instantly blistered by the poisonous latex that is released.

All this, a paradise and hell in confusing parallels, belonged only to the Amerindians for nearly 2,000 years. Travelling from their ancestral home in the Orinoco river region, in what is now known as Guyana and Venezuela on the South American mainland, the Arawaks had come first to the southernmost islands of Trinidad and Tobago in the third century BC, having worked their way out of the Orinoco river basin in dug-out canoes up to 27m in length. Wave after wave of immigrants followed to settle in the land they called 'Irie', the land of the humming bird. The Arawaks were peaceful people who, by AD 650, had reached as far as Jamaica. Some centuries later their calm style of living in the islands was disrupted. War was raged on them by the Caribs who, it is thought, came from the same region, and many were murdered before the arrival of the Europeans.

The Indians were superb seamen who kept their expanding tendencies within sensible limits, working their way up the archipelago of islands from mainland Guiana to Cuba. Many of these islands were formed by volcanic eruption, and the Indians used them as a navigational aid, keeping a close eye on the topmost peak of each island as they canoed. They believed that the peak was inhabited by their dead chief and they took the conical shape as a symbol, which they called a 'cemis', often sculpting it in small stone forms.

They travelled in great faith, for they believed the very seas that bore them through the heaving troughs of indigo waters northward were created when their mythological Father Yaya placed the bones of his rebellious son, whom he had murdered, in the branches of the calabaza tree. This extreme action spawned the heavenly waters of the world and filled them with all the creatures imaginable.

Two attitudes prevailed amongst the Europeans. One was that the Amerindians were savage cannibals; rumours of their practices abounded. Indeed, cannibalism took its name from the Caribs. Anthropologists now say there is no evidence of their being eaters of human flesh, but it is thought that they practised some forms of ritual sampling of the parts of beloved chieftains or enemies. An English historian once wrote of the Carib practice: 'Spanish flesh causes indigestion, the French were too delicate in taste, whilst the English were too tough.' It seems probable that this myth began with the Spaniards, who used claims of 'unhumanly' cannibalism to ensure that the laws for the enslavement of the Amerindian would be sanctioned. Four natives whom they had captured 'had had their virile members cut off'. Spanish imagination would have it that they had been castrated, 'as we do fatten capons, to improve their taste . . . guts and limbs eaten and the rest salted and dried like our hams'.

The other view, that the Indians were romantic primitives, is much easier to sustain. In the dim coolness of the local museum in the West Indian island of Grenada, there is a pathetic collection of objects hinting at the existence of the many peoples who had been here. On a few cards, fading quickly as all things do in the humidity of the tropics, are translations of the words that have survived from the language of the lost indigenous Amerindian civilization. The poignancy of their vivid language almost wrings the heart; they were jewels of creativity.

'Soul of the hand' meant pulse, 'God's plume of feathers', rainbow and 'my heart', wife. Saddest is the translation that showed their perception of the European as the 'misshapen enemy'.

Of course, neither of these European views approach the reality. The Indian lived with himself as the centre of his world, and his god, Yocahu, was morally indifferent to the dreams and hopes of his followers. Just before daybreak the village *shaman*, who acted as a doctor-priest for the Indians, would address the ancestral spirits. Then the Indians would join him, augmenting the bemoaning of the departed ones with a noise commensurate with their fear that the spirits might return and take vengeance for not receiving appropriate tributes to their greatness. Only as the sun rose were their fears vanquished.

There were many accounts by Spanish conquistador historians, and later by Englishmen such as Drake and Raleigh, of their encounters with the Indians. Indian settlements were found scattered across the islands. Each was led by a *cacique* or chief. In the clearings of the forests they built their huts, grouped around an open plaza which was used for ceremonies. Their homes were made of mud and wattle and the roofs were supported by four posts, plaited with palm leaves. Nearby in smaller clearings were plantings of cassava and maize.

There is both written and archaeological evidence of the Amerindians' extraordinarily intimate knowledge of fishing, hunting and gathering along the swampy coastal regions. If you know where to look, you can find their tools made of bone, stone and shell, which have remained like fingerprints in the earth. Recent excavations of some kitchen middens, the village refuse heaps, have shown that the Amerindians were accustomed to catching over forty varieties of different fish, and were all too familiar with the same diet of seafood that we enjoy today: bones and shells of the grouper, parrotfish, sturgeon, shark, lobster, oyster conch, whelk, oyster and crab have been found. The Indians enjoyed the green part of the crab meat in the shell and used to mix it with lime juice, making a sauce called *tamaulin* to eat with cassava bread. This is the first evidence I have found of seasoning food with lime juice in the islands, a habit later adopted by nearly all newcomers in turn, whatever their country of origin. Much of the wild meat and fish, such as shark, is still prepared by marinading or washing in water and fresh lime juice, because the taste is 'too fresh or strong' when just caught. In the north we rarely experience meat or fish just brought in and have no need of this stage.

The earth's natural beauty and freshness was their daily experience on such fishing and hunting trips. One traveller to Guyana wrote of the Amerindians' habitat:

> ... the dark red, wine-coloured water runs arched over by gigantic trees and palms. The swampy banks are thickly set with ferns, and large lily-leaved aroids. At the water's edge a carpet of half transparent filmy ferns and mosses keep it continually moist ... there is no colour and the air is cool, almost chilly. But in one place, where a tree has fallen and left a space in the forest roof, the glorious and intensely blue sky appeared, its colour thrown into extraordinary vividness by a wreath of a scarlet-blossomed passion flower which had thrown itself across the open space from tree to tree.

Along the banks of the rivers and streams, the colour was introduced by the occasional flash of kingfishers, parrots, toucans and the scarlet ibis.

The men would only fish or hunt in parties. Their fishing techniques were quite ingenious. For the rocky pools and streams inland, they would prepare delicately-fashioned arrowheads with poison to shoot the fish. Alternatively, they would poison the stream waters with narcotic juices from local plants and stupefy, but not kill, the fish. Or, if heavy rains were clouding the waters of the rivers and streams, they would make woven wicker baskets to put into the water with a bait inside that the fish particularly liked. They then preserved them by slitting the flesh and rubbing in salt, of which they were especially fond. They obtained their supplies from the Savannah where it occurred naturally and used it for bartering; later they procured it from the English.

A fourth technique was to dam the flow of the waters, either with boulders or by driving stakes into the stream bed and interweaving them to form a fibrous wall. Any fish which managed to escape these methods would be picked up by the men on the banks.

Where the Amerindian lived close to the sea, he could pluck all that he needed from the sea floor or from the skies above. He hunted birds by immersing himself in the water, covering his head with a large calabash to disguise himself. As the bird alighted on the surface, he would grab its legs and pull it under. Close to the shore, he could pull up lobsters from the sea floor for they came into the shallows to breed.

It would seem that the Amerindian's preparation of fish and meat was very simple, sticking to the raw ingredients almost invariably roasted over an open fire. On his travels he always carried a firebrand with him so that he could stop and cook whatever he had caught straight away. The finest lobster I have ever eaten was picked out of the sea and roasted in the Amerindian way. We lit a small wood fire, chopped the creature in two lengthways, then removed the head and the digestive tract and stomach. By now the wood had burnt down, leaving hot glowing coals. We laid the two sides of the lobster, shell-side down, on a wire grill over the fire. Depending on how well done you like the meat, you could leave it there for between five and ten minutes. This method keeps the succulence of the flesh perfectly and is indescribably good.

We began this meal with roasted sea eggs, exactly like those dived for in the West Country in England. They abound around the shores of the West Indian islands, where they are considered a great delicacy, and are sold to tourists, ready to eat, steaming hot and delicious in the shell.

I was taught how to prepare them by a local who was called a black Carib – that is, someone with mixed African and Amerindian blood. They are far and few between now, but they are unmistakable in appearance. Their features are usually Amerindian and their skin-colour and hair are Negro in type.

I met the Carib one day in Dominica on the beach. He had just returned from collecting sea eggs from the reef and was cleaning them. He broke a hole in the top of each round shell and shook out the watery stomach contents. Into a pot of sea water he scraped out the eggs, which adhere in narrow strips of up to 5 cm long and 1 cm wide, a little apart all around the inside of the shell. These he washed, removing any bits of seaweed, then stuffed the eggs back into one shell – he used at least forty strips of eggs – until they burgeoned in a yellow cornmeal-coloured mass over the top. Placing them near to the fire in the hot ashes, he turned them regularly until the short whitish-grey spines turned brown. Finally he turned the top to the fire to form a crust, scraped off the now brittle spines and handed us one each.

We ate them straight, just as they were, with a teaspoon, and had the sense that this rich abundance of food in one shell, and the amount of time and work it took to collect so many sea eggs to fill just one shell, was a luxury that one would not see for very much longer. After his long day's work, which was not without its dangers, the Carib ended up roasting only five eggs in the fire. Each of the full eggs he was selling for a mere pound.

If you find such a concentration of flavour, which is comparable to the strong exotic taste of the oyster, too rich, take them home and prepare in the following way.

 1–2 **Sea Eggs** will be enough for a first course for four people. Fry some shallots or a little crushed garlic in unsalted butter. When soft, scrape the eggs out of the shell and stir gently in the pan until they are warmed through. Try a squeeze of lime on it. Or, if absolutely fresh, they are best eaten raw. Allow one per person. Break a hole in the top of them and shake out the watery content, scoop out the yellow strips of eggs with a spoon, look up at the waving heads of the palms, breathe in the fresh salt air, and swallow. Sip a good chilled white wine such as Pinot d'Alsace in-between each mouthful.

In the Windward Islands on the remoter beaches on the Atlantic side of the island, piles of very sun-bleached white conch shells are heaped either at one end of a beach or just inshore. They were part of the Indians' daily food. We do not know how they prepared them, but probably they shelled and roasted them or boiled them in sea water. Later the fresh pink-pearled shells supplied Victorian England with the base from which they carved ornate cameos.

The Indians must have taught the settlers how to take the meat out and clean it, for it is almost impossible to discover, unless you are shown how. First you count down from the tip to the third or fourth space on the helix, where you will find a flat surface. Insert a sharp knife or instrument into the shell here, cutting 8 cm long and 3 cm wide. Push the knife through the shell and cut into the ligament that holds the creature solidly to the shell wall. It will then pull out easily, although it is slimy and slippery at this stage. Failing such a stout heart, I have been advised to put the creature in its shell in cold water, bring to the boil and simmer for thirty minutes; it will then pull out easily and you can strain the water and use it for stock. After you have taken off the slime with lots of pumpkin leaves or lime juice, the meat needs as much pounding as octopus. Try putting it in a rough canvas cloth to hold it while you 'pong it good', as they say, then skin it, removing any little hard black bits on the tips, for the appearance would put some people off.

The early English settlers liked conch soused, which is a refreshing dish for hot weather. Today it is also locally called *lambie*. It has been passed down through the generations and is now used to prepare several varieties of fish; you could substitute monkfish, rockhind or octopus. The souse seasoning is very much a question of taste, so when you make it for the first time, keep testing until you find a balance you like, especially while you are adding the lime juice. It should only be made just before you intend to eat it, since you want the seasonings to be a crisp contrast to the fish.

To make **Lambie Souse** as a first course for four, you will need to allow 100–125 g (4 oz) of conch meat prepared as above (you may substitute monkfish or rockhind), 2–3 shallots, very finely sliced so that they are transparent, ½ a peeled cucumber, ½ a green pepper, again thinly sliced, 1 deseeded and thinly chopped red seasoning pepper, the juice of a large fresh lime, salt and pepper to taste, and a touch of crisp watercress. Cut up the conch meat into small cubes, put into cold water, bring to the boil and simmer until it is soft. (If you are using the other fish, skin, fillet and cut into small pieces, steam for a minute or two.) Allow to cool, then mix all the ingredients together in a glass bowl and add the conch (or fish pieces) and the watercress.

Locals often say that when the colour of the ocean around the islands deepens to a strange cobalt blue, as it does at certain times of year, it has been changed by the flood waters of one of the world's most powerful rivers, the Orinoco. The flood waters build up from deep in the South American jungle and burst through the waters of the Atlantic with such force that the flood streams reach Trinidad undissipated, and sometimes Grenada some ninety miles to the north. The banks of the Orinoco are low with occasional mud flats and here, and on the southern shores of Trinidad, you will find an extraordinary creature called the cascadura, which dwells in the mud. It is from the Silurian age and has all the appearance of a primaeval mud-dweller, with a scaly armour-plated shell and partly developed lungs.

Today the cascadura has become a favourite with East Indian Trinidadians, who love it so well that they have it shipped to restaurants in London. It needs washing thoroughly in copious amounts of fresh running water until the mud is removed. For while the taste, when cooked, is faintly muddy, it can be overdone. It can be boiled very simply or put over some hot coals and cooked like the roasted lobster, but in the Caribbean today it is usually stewed or curried.

One of the Amerindians' most ingenious fishing techniques was used for the green turtle, of which they were very fond. They realized that a certain fish called the remora or suckerfish fed by attaching itself to sharks or other large fish, such as the big blue parrotfish, by a sucker the size of a large plate on its forehead. The Arawak would catch the remora, feed and tame it, then accustom it to carrying a light cord tied to its tail and gill frame. When a turtle came near to their canoe, they released the remora, which would swim to the turtle and suck on its carapace. Then they could haul it into the boat.

Of course the turtle appealed very much to the settlers also; one traveller wrote: '. . . there is the green turtle which is of a lesser magnitude, but far exceeding others in wholesomeness and rareness of taste.' Apart from going to sea to catch the turtle, they enjoyed it as much when it came ashore of its own volition twice a year and laid its eggs in the sand banks along the rivers. Curiously, the Indians would not eat the eggs from their hens or birds, but relished those of the turtle, iguana and (less common) the tortoise. Large groups of them would go down to the shore to collect the eggs, which would often weigh down the canoes almost to the edge of the water. The eggs would be pickled, smoked or dried; this way they kept for a considerable length of time. If they are eaten fresh – and they need to be very fresh – they are boiled and the albumen is expressed, leaving only the deliciously buttery yolk. The Caribs also boiled the musk-flavoured eggs of the Caymen alligator, a habit looked on with disgust by the Arawaks.

Amerindian life was coloured richly by legends. They believed that when they first arrived on earth from the 'sky land', all the vegetables and fruit they needed grew on one tree, from which the tapir fed himself. The land they had arrived in had very poor soil and yielded little but they noticed that the tapir was living very well, so they set the woodpecker to follow him to discover the source of his food. However, the woodpecker gave himself away by the noise he made gorging on the insects on the tree. Then they sent a rat who bargained with the tapir and they agreed to share, but the rat was so greedy that the Indians found him sleeping with his mouth still full of corn, and so they forced him to take them to the tree. After many months work, they felled the tree and each man took away a piece to plant for his own.

Other legends show us that the first explorers to the new world must have talked extensively with the natives; animals from other continents that they could never have seen, such as the elephant, were perfectly described in their mythology. The hunters would tell of the time when their ancestors lived in the 'sky land'. One of those ancestors was the famous hunter Okonorote. He followed a bird for many days without managing to shoot it. At length his arrow pierced the bird, it fell to earth into a deep pit and was lost. When Okonorote looked into the pit he saw daylight and a land where four-footed animals walked, so his fellow hunters lowered him on a long rope towards the earth and he climbed down. After successful hunting he returned with some venison. So great was the appreciation of this unusual food that the rest of the tribe vowed to move through the hole to the earth, which they did until the hole was blocked by an enormously fat woman and the exodus came to an end.

Whatever the moral of this tale, venison there was in plenty on the islands. Richard Ligon, who voyaged to the Caribbean in the middle of the sixteenth century and recorded his findings in great detail, said that such meat was boiled in clay pots so finely made and tempered that even in England he had not seen such 'fineness of mettle and curiosity of turning'. I remember once, when sitting on a remote beach near the old airport in Grenada, local children offered us shards of Arawak pottery of quite beautiful shapes and design, from an archaeological dig close by. These shapes were enhanced by the rich dyes of reds and orange made from local plants.

Argument about such pots found in Barbados raged hotly in the middle of the sixteenth century. On his return to England, Ligon found himself a prisoner in the Upper Bench prison in the company of an ancient Captain Canon who had been one of those first to land in Barbados. The Captain insisted that the pots were brought later by the African, but Ligon stuck to his view – and that of the planters – because, he said, the Indian often sailed his canoe to Barbados: 'finding such game to hunt, as these hogs and the flesh so sweet and excellent in taste, they often came thither a hunting'.

There are many accounts of plentiful supplies of deer; being wild, the creatures probably would have been quite tough. Whatever the truth of the matter, they certainly ate and appreciated the venison later hunted by the European settlers. In their recipes, marinading was said to be essential. Porter, thought to have been very close in taste to Guinness, was as popular in the West Indies as in England in the eighteenth century, and was a useful tenderizer of meat. Today Guinness can be used; it behaves in the final tasting of the cooked dish like an excellent wine.

To make **Guinness Stew** for four people take ½ kg (1 lb) of venison and dice it into small cubes, leave it to marinade for two to three hours in 250 ml (8 fl oz) of Guinness. Apart from this, you will need 1 pig's foot, 1 large mild onion, 1–2 cloves of crushed garlic, olive oil, salt and black pepper to taste, a pinch of thyme, another 250 ml (8 fl oz) of good meat stock (preferably game), 1 teaspoon of demerara sugar and 1 tablespoon of red wine vinegar. Drain the marinade off the meat, throw out the marinade and dry the cubes of meat. Dice the onions very finely and fry them with the crushed garlic in olive oil. When they are quite soft, add the meat and chopped pig's foot, the salt, black pepper and thyme, and stir well. Cook over a high heat for a few minutes. Lower the heat and cover with a good lid. Let the meat sweat out its juices for fifteen to twenty minutes, then add the remaining ingredients and meat stock and top up with Guinness to cover the meat. Cook for at least an hour and a half, the time depending on the quality of the cut you have bought. It may take two hours or more – the longer the better, to allow the gelatinous quality of the pig's foot to thicken the stew. If there is too much liquid, reduce over a fast heat. A touch of Dijon mustard is an improvement. Serve with plain boiled white rice.

Hunting was the most important part of the male Indian's life; his rank in the village depended on his skill in the chase. He applied a variety of excruciating tortures to himself and his dogs before setting off, to ensure that they would not flinch at the kill. As they hunted through the countryside they collected land tortoises – which they carried home alive and kept in pens – birds, eggs and animals. What they did not eat to sustain them for the hunt, they preserved for the long journey home by smoking them on a *brabacot*, a platform of green sticks made of animal hides and bones, built over a fire. On this the meat was laid to expose it to the smoke.

This smoking was not to be the final cooking of the meat; that was done by the women when they returned home. The hunters would send smoke signals as they approached the village to alert the women to prepare cassava bread, and would hand over their meats before falling into their hammocks where they stayed for as many days as they had been hunting to recover. Here the women would hand them pieces of smoked meat to sustain them.

The Caribs showed the first Spanish colonists how to smoke-dry in this way on the island of Hispaniola. The Spanish adapted *brabacot*, the Indian name for the green wood lattices, to *barbacao*, and from this grew the art of barbecuing. The meat cooked was usually pork –

often from wild hogs whose flesh was tasty but tough – which was called *boucan* once it was smoked. In Jamaica a special combination of seasonings, closely resembling that for jerk pork, was used to rub into the flesh first.

Jamaican **Boucan** can be done on an ordinary grill over some very hot coals. Choose your pork carefully. The side of the pig, using the ribs, is best. To make the seasoning, which is really excellent, you will need 4–5 spring onions, 1 small sprig of French thyme, 1 medium head of garlic, 250 g (8 oz) chopped onions, 25 g (1 oz) freshly ground allspice berries, 25 g (1 oz) fresh ginger and 2 tablespoons of olive oil. Add the minimum of water to blend all this to a paste. These quantities will make 750 g (1½ lbs) of seasoning. Use 500 g (1 lb) to season half a pig weighing approximately 5 kg (11 lbs).The rest will keep for some weeks in the refrigerator. An hour or two before you want to cook the pork, cut pieces of your choice, salt and rub the seasoning in for an hour or two. In fact, the seasoning is so good that you can rub it in straight away and put it over the fire without the preliminary marinading. Good pork should be done in at least thirty minutes.

Other animals known to have been on the islands include the guinea pig, which the Indian took with him when he left the mainland, and the agouti. This creature was very much appreciated as a delicacy and was rather like a rice rat, which lived on nuts, roots and fruits. The Indians also increased the protein in their diet by eating all kinds of grubs such as ants, termites, caterpillars and a beetle grub called 'gru gru worm', or *ewoi* by the Caribs and *tacooma* by the Arawaks, a delicacy which was much appreciated by the early Europeans and later the Africans.

All these were hunted and later sold to the settlers. Aphra Behn, a young woman who travelled through the Caribbean in her early twenties and who was described some three centuries later by Vita Sackville-West as 'the first English woman to earn her living by the pen', wrote in her seventeenth-century autobiographical novel *Oroonoko*, which focused on an enslaved African prince:

. . . those they make use of there not being natives of the place: for those we live with in perfect amity, without daring to command 'em, but on the contrary, caress 'em with all brotherly affection in the world: trading with them for their fish and venison. The very meat when set upon the table, if it be native, perfumes the whole room.

The meat they would have used if it were to be native of the place, would have been tatoo which was an armadillo, agouti which was like a rabbit with long legs, bush hogs and labba which were large guinea pigs. During the hunt when the Indian had caught an animal, he would half smoke it and consume the entire creature, no matter what size it was, often frustrating the European if he was hunting with him, for nothing would move him on till he was done; they dreaded each new catch, for it would produce a repeat performance.

When the first eighty settlers arrived in Barbados with Captain Powell, the island was deserted save for a few hogs left by an earlier passing Portuguese ship. Although they had been specially hand-picked for their youth and strength to cope with the problems of tree-felling and digging the land, it was immediately apparent that they needed extra help to establish themselves. Powell, therefore, sailed off to the neighbouring colony of Guyana on the South American mainland to persuade a Dutch friend to give him forty Arawak Indians whom he could enslave and take back to Barbados to teach local ways with building shelter, planting and general survival. Without the knowledge of the Indians, the settlers would not have survived for a moment.

The first English settlers had arrived in Barbados in 1627 at the inspiration of a new breed of English merchant prince. Sir William Courteen, son of a Dutch refugee, had so endeared himself to James I that he was granted a royal charter 'with power to discover . . . and plant colonies therein'. On an earlier expedition to South America he had found the island of Barbados to be uninhabited by other Europeans and an ideal place to develop the tobacco plantations. The Lord Treasurer recommended Courteen to James I as a 'man who deserved to be respected . . . in regard he so willinglie and freelie lends his money for supplie of his Majesty's occaisions and that, with out the interest of the old debt . . .' The climate in Court and City circles was also greatly in favour of the new tobacco planting schemes.

The most important foodstuff that the Europeans found in the Caribbean was maize, derived from the Arawak-Carib name *mahiz*. The settlers' very survival depended on it, for one head of corn could feed one man for a day. Problems of fascinating complexity are raised today of whether or not maize did in fact reach the Old World in pre-Columbian times. Nevertheless, Columbus, on reaching Cuba, said: 'It was the most tasty boiled, roasted or ground into flour.' The English settlers put the Arawaks to plant maize for them straightaway, and it was the task of the Indians to choose a good site. Barbados was ideal.

They were set to fell the trees and, when the weather was dry, to burn all the trunks and heavy branches. The fires smouldered for many days and when at last they died out, there was a clearing in the forest, its floor white with ashes. Some trees remained standing where their bark had fallen, the exposed trunks white and glistening silver. Others were charred and blackened and the clearing had the appearance of a moonscape.

Although the Indians knew how to grow fruit and vegetables successfully, it was done in a very disorganized way to Western eyes. The settlers found the crops growing 'straggling amongst the woods with some other fruits; for the woods were so thick and most of the trees so large and massive'.

Nonetheless, so successful were the Indians, despite the haphazard approach to planting, that the settlers ate their first corn within three months. From this, the Indians showed them how to make 'lob-lolly', now thought of as ship's gruel, and described in early records as crushed maize and water. This, I believe, is the forerunner of *cou-cou*, the dish now looked upon with much affection by the modern Bajan, who thickened and refined it by adding okras and eggs.

The Italian traveller, Benzoni, who recorded much that he saw between 1541 and 1556, observed the Indian women preparing the ripened corn by wetting 'a small quantity of grain the previous evening with cold water and in the morning they grind it between two stones. Some stand up to it, others kneel on the ground. When they have made a mass by sprinkling water with the hand, they shape it into little loaves, either long or round and putting in some leaves of reeds, with as little water as possible, they cook them.' It apparently lasted two days or so before becoming mildewed.

I have read accounts of the very sophisticated method the Indians employed for making steamed corn using their form of a bain-marie with two clay pots. The crushed corn meal was sifted, moistened with water and put into one of the clay pots which was placed into the other that was filled with water. It was then steamed until soft. Alternatively, having moistened the meal enough to make it into a dough, they wrapped small pieces of it into corn husks and baked them on the live coals or hot ashes and ate them hot. I imagine this to be very good indeed and I have never found a record of the settlers preparing corn any way except as bread. Ligon recorded that the early settlers quickly learned to make three different kinds of bread from the crops of corn, potato and cassava that the Indians cultivated, for the flour they brought from England tended not to last and was full of weevils. 'Bread, which is accounted the staff of life, or main supporter of man's life, has not here that full taste it has in England,' wrote one visitor. Nevertheless, it was probably excellent, for the English learned to build wood ovens the shape and size of an igloo. They were made from local stone and plastered with clay. A fire was built inside and when the oven was heated enough and too close to stand near, they removed the fire and everyone who lived nearby would come with their pans of bread. These ovens are still in use and are preferred by many in country areas to this day. The cakes and bread baked in them are superb and are cooked in all of fifteen minutes.

To make the **Corn Bread,** which is very good and also good for you because of the high fibre content, you will need 90 g (3 oz) of very finely ground yellow cornflour, 125 ml (4 fl oz) of boiling water, 1½ teaspoons of salt, 500 g (16 oz) of white flour, 15 g (½ oz) of easy-blend yeast, 1 teaspoon of white sugar, 125 ml (4 fl oz) of warm milk, 125 ml (4 fl oz) of warm water and 30g (1 oz) of butter. Put the corn meal in a saucepan and pour the boiling water over it. Cook for six to eight minutes with ½ teaspoon of salt; keep stirring so that it does not stick, then spread over a large plate to cool. Put the flour, yeast, 1 teaspoon each of salt and sugar in a large bowl, mix in the barely warmed milk, add the cooled corn and begin mixing together, adding the warmed water a little at a time to make the dough. The amount of water varies according to the coarseness of the corn meal. At first it may look as if the corn meal won't mix in evenly; try to break it up into small pieces as you add it to the flour, but the kneading will distribute it perfectly if you do it for at least ten minutes. I would check the dough for salt and add more if needed. Coat the dough when it is kneaded with the butter and leave to rise. Sometimes the dough is a little sticky when you punch it down for the second time, so sprinkle the board with an extra 15–30 g (½–1 oz) of flour as you knead it, then put into the baking tin and leave it to rise again. Pre-heat the oven and cook the bread at 220°C (425°F, Gas mark 7) for ten minutes, then lower the temperature to 180°C (350°F, Gas mark 4) for another twenty to twenty-five minutes. Leave to cool, then remove from tin.

Butter would not often have been used in this recipe in the very early years of settlement. It was said that if you did not have a cow, then it was best to use butter that travelled out from England or Holland on a ship that would set sail from England in November and arrive in

Barbados in mid-December: 'When the sun is at its furthest distance, the butter may come thither in a very good condition.'

Potato bread was, by all accounts, good too, for the potato lightened the texture. Since baker's yeast was not manufactured until the nineteenth century, it meant that the bread makers always had to rely on keeping back a small piece of fermented dough after the day's baking was done, which was used to ferment the next batch. Even today, in some parts of the West Indies, older people will remember making bread in this way and preferring it, calling it leaven bread, or sourdough bread. Elizabeth David recommends a very good recipe in her remarkable book on English bread.

 For **Potato Bread** you will need 120 g (4 oz) of cooked potatoes, 15 g (½ oz) of dried yeast, a pinch of sugar, 450 g (14 oz) of plain white flour, 20 g (¾ oz) of salt and 280 ml (9 fl oz) of milk and water mixed together. The potatoes used should be old and floury English potatoes, boiled whole, then peeled, sieved and kept warm (not hot) until ready to use. While preparing the potatoes, cream the yeast with a little warm water and a pinch of sugar. Using a large bowl, put the flour and salt in with the potatoes. By now the yeast will have become frothy; make a well in the centre of the flour and add the yeast with the milk and water. Mix it into a dough as you would ordinary bread and leave to rise – covered with a damp cloth (to help prevent a skin forming) – which Elizabeth David says may take up to two hours. Punch down lightly and press into an oiled bread tin. Bake in a moderately hot oven (220°C, 425°F, Gas mark 7) for forty-five minutes.

Cassava or manioc is better known in the north as tapioca and was the other vital crop that the settlers needed to learn to make their bread from. There are two kinds of cassava: one is called 'sweet' and the other 'bitter'. Even today there are many who cannot tell the difference, for the roots of the shrubs are a fibrous dark brown and although the shapes can differ considerably, they otherwise look much the same. The sweet cassava can be peeled and even eaten raw, but the bitter variety has lethal quantities of prussic acid which has to be extracted before eating it.

It was to the Indians, whose enormous knowledge and understanding of the world they lived in and the ability to solve the problem of which cassava to use and how to grow and prepare it, that the settlers owed much of their survival.

As the rainy season started and the rains began to fall, the women would loosen small patches of soil and insert three or four sticks of cassava. They would weed from time to time, but only enough to prevent the cultivated plants from being strangled. Wherever space was left, the women would plant all kinds of root crops, from sweet potatoes to yams, pineapple tops, pumpkin and water-melon seeds. Above all this, and shading everything from the sun, grew banana and plantain stools, sugar-cane and pawpaw trees, all to heights of about four metres. Below, smaller bushes of red and yellow pepper trees grew. The colour, profusion and confusion must have been a fabulous sight to a newcomer's uninitiated eye. For the ten months the cassava took to reach maturity, every kind of wild flower twined itself around the stems, from the large and purple passion flower to the convolvulus with its mist-blue face.

Preparing cassava for bread or farina was a painstaking and very time-consuming task, and every house in the village would have been occupied with some part of the preparations. The women would dig up the cassava roots as they needed them, taking cuttings as they went and replanting them in the same hole. The rest of the work was divided. Some women would peel and wash the brown hairy root, others would then scrape the roots up and down on an oblong board on which small chips of granite were embedded in a strong black vegetable pitch. A traveller through Guyana left a description of the laborious work: 'One end of the grater stood in a trough in the ground, the other rested against the women's knees; it is violent exercise. As the woman scrapes, her body swings down and up again from the hips.' The characteristic sounds of the grating and rhythmical swishing meant that the village was alive and well, the harvest had been a success and everyone would survive.

The pulp from the grated cassava, which was highly poisonous at this stage, was collected and put in a *matapie*, a cleverly woven cylinder that hung from the roof. To the bottom of the *matapie* they attached a loop, through which they passed a very heavy pole weighted to the ground at one end by large stones. The women would then pull the other end towards the ground, thus stretching the weave to make the cylinder longer and narrower and forcing out the poisonous juices. The pulp left behind, now entirely safe, was sieved into a meal, dried out in the sun and made at once into bread, or stored in banana leaves for later use.

Other women would make the clay pots and cassava griddles for baking the bread. Ligon wrote that, with some difficulty, the settlers on Barbados persuaded Indians to come from the neighbouring island of

St Vincent to help them make pots that would not burn or break. To begin with, the settlers used the Indian clay griddle or pone, as they called it, spreading out a thin layer of the meal and pressing it into a thin round pancake on the griddle, which they then put over the fire. 'When they think that side almost well enough, they so turn and return until enough,' wrote Ligon. The flames were fanned by the women with their hands; in a few minutes the bread would be done. They then threw it on to the thatched roof of their houses to dry in the sun. Today it is sometimes called *bammie*.

The Indians' way of preparing the cassava was described by N. Fernandez Enciso, the author of *A Brief Summe of Geographie*. He noticed that when the cassava had been prepared, 'ther resteth in the bagge the floure as fyne and white as the snow, whereof thei make cakys and bake them upon the fier in a panne.' He went on to say that it was so 'holsome and medicinable, and will endure a yere without corruptying'.

Cassava is much more interesting mixed with coconut. The combination makes a delicious cake. To make **Cassava Cake with Coconut** you will need 100–125 g (4 oz) each of white sugar and unsalted butter, 4 large separated eggs, 500 g (1 lb) of dried cassava (this can now be bought already grated or frozen), 2 tablespoons of plain flour, 2 tablespoons of baking powder, and 120 g (4 oz) of dessicated coconut. Mix the butter and sugar to a cream, beat the egg yolk and mix in. Fold in the cassava, flour and baking powder with the coconut. Mix this into a thick paste; you may need to add a little water if it seems too thick, since the cassava can vary in its degree of dryness. Beat the egg whites until they are stiff and fold into a mixture. Put into a baking tin and place in a pre-heated hot oven for fifteen minutes, then put on to the lowest shelf for another ten minutes, turning the oven right down, or off altogether.

The poisonous juice which had been wrung out from the cassava was boiled until it became a thick black treacle-like substance called cassareep. The Indians had learned many centuries before that when fresh meat was dropped into it, it was preserved, and that they could keep adding more meat and reboiling it every day, much as you would do with a *pot-au-feu*. This is how the women finished the cooking of the smoked or brabacoted game while the men lay in their hammocks for many days recovering from the strains of the hunt.

Pepperpot, a dish which developed from this Amerindian way of cooking meat with cassareep, has remained a favourite to this day in many of the islands and, according to legend, has been known to continue for a hundred years or more. We recently lunched at an old plantation home where we were told that pepperpot had been on the menu every day for the last twelve years, uninterrupted, except on the day the Americans 'intervened'. Also, in the former days when life on the estates was running at full tilt and horses and mules were the only form of transport, the grand plantation houses would be regularly called upon to feed travellers who had to stay overnight, so a constant supply of ready food was necessary. The *canaree*, an enormous earthenware pot blackened with age, was wrapped with fresh white napkins and magnificently placed on the great mahogany sideboards each day at luncheon. From its steaming savoury depths could be drawn a delicious miscellany of stewed meats. It is unlikely that you will find the cassareep to do it in the north; it is an ancient dish that kept many hungry people fed, while building up the island estates to produce the 'white gold' – sugar.

For **Grenada Pepperpot** for six to eight people you may use any amount of different meats but do not use onions or garlic, the locals say, 'for it will turn sour'. I did, but froze the finished dish successfully. Upon reheating, there seemed to be no change and it was almost as good. I put 750 g (1½ lbs) of silver side of beef, 1 pig's trotter and a hock and 1 kg (2 lbs) of oxtail into a large pot. I marinaded this in 125–150 ml (4–5 fl oz) of cassareep overnight. The next morning I added a rough piece of cinnamon bark of 2.5 cm (1 inch) in length, a tablespoon of brown demerara sugar, 6 cloves, 2 bay or pimento or clove leaves, 1 hot pepper, 500 g (1 lb) of finely chopped mild onion and a head of garlic cut horizontally in two. I covered this with 1.2 l (2 pints) of cold water and brought it to the boil, then let it simmer for two and a half hours. I felt that the cassareep I was given smelt and tasted suspiciously like molasses; it is more than likely you could achieve something similar using half the amount of molasses.

Cassava was also used to make *perino*, an Indian drink that the settlers gratefully adopted as 'the likest to English beer of any drink we have there'. The root was given to old wives who had very few remaining teeth to 'chaw', and they then spat it into water 'for the better breaking and macerating of the root'. It was reckoned that the old women's breath was so poisonous and 'their teeth tainted with many several poxs . . . such opposites to the poison of the cassava, that they bend their forces vehemently against one another and spend their poisons in that conflict'. Any remaining impurities were thought to be cast out by the water that was very pure, since the rain filtered down into subterranean caverns; the settlers learned to sink boreholes to recover it. Whatever the real science behind such a primitive process, it did make a beer that kept for up to a month. Until beer began to be imported, the Europeans were glad enough to adopt the Amerindian drinks.

Another drink was known as 'mobbie', from the Carib-Indian word *mabi*. Richard Ligon, our travel writer of the 1600s, described it as a potato beer, not mentioning that the potatoes were in fact sweet, although he described them as being either red or green. Having been scrubbed, they were transferred to a large brass pot and enough water was added to cover a 'quarter part of them'. Double canvas was fitted over the pot to prevent the steam escaping as the fire was lit below. The potatoes were squeezed and mashed in 'fair water and kept for an hour or two so that the spirit of the root was sucked out. The remaining mash was then placed in a jelly bag and dript for twenty four hours'. Ligon likened the end result to a 'Rhenish wine in the must', red as a claret wine if they used the red variety, but added a precautionary note that he thought it caused 'hydropic rumours'.

The settlers seem to have spent a large amount of time and energy making sure there were enough alcoholic drinks available. When the first recipes for punches appeared, they were simple sugar and water syrups left to stand for ten days until they were exceedingly strong. Today a syrup is still used as the basis of all punches, but the alcohol – usually rum – is added later. To make this **syrup for punch** add 500 g (1 lb) white sugar to 125–150 ml (4–5 fl oz) of water and dissolve over a moderate heat stirring all the time, then bring to the boil for another ten minutes. Allow it to cool, bottle and keep it in the refrigerator.

 **Falernum,** invented a little later and still a traditional drink in Barbados today, seems to me to be a more sophisticated version of the punch. Apparently, if left to mature for six months or more, it is delicious. I use the following recipe by Sylvia Hunt. You will need 250 ml (8 fl oz) water, 500 g (1 lb) white sugar, 250 ml (8 fl oz) fresh lime juice, 500 ml (16 fl oz) of rum and 4 drops of almond essence. Bring the water to the boil and slowly stir in the sugar until it has dissolved, cool and blend with the remaining ingredients. Store in a very cool dark place for six months and serve on lots of crushed ice.

The Indians also loved to drink. Raleigh called them the greatest carousers in the world and loved to join them. The Arawaks believed that the sun and the moon were associated with their two supreme gods,

Jocuahuma and his female counterpart. They also maintained that man had emerged from a cave and when he departed from this life, he would go to a place of ease, where he would no longer be threatened by natural disasters such as hurricanes, drought, sickness or the menace of slavery. They called it *Coyaba*; a place of rest where the time could be spent feasting and dancing.

Marriages and funerals were often occasions for a feast; other times there was no special reason. When they held a *Paiwari* feast, invitations were sent to all the neighbouring settlements where the Indians were from the same tribe. The guests would all be involved in the bread-making and hunting for meat and fish. Almost every house had a wooden *paiwari*, which was a wooden trough, standing in the centre of each hut and shaped like a canoe, which held from 150 to 200 gallons of *perino*. The women would prepare it a day or so in advance to allow it to mellow and ferment. All the guests would bring their hammocks and every spare calabash to use as drinking cups. For days they would consume enormous amounts, making themselves sick every so often, so that they could start again.

Four hundred years later **Pine Wine** is still made. I use this very simple recipe by Sylvia Hunt. Peel a good ripe unblemished pineapple. When peeled, the flesh should weigh 1.5kg (3 lbs). Remove the eyes, then cut the flesh up into small chunks. Put the pieces with 250 g (8 oz) of raisins into a large earthenware jar and pour 5 litres (8 pints) of boiling water over them. Cover with a clean cloth with a small hole in the centre. Leave in a cool dark place for two days, then add 2 teaspoons of dry yeast and 1.5 kg (3 lbs) of white sugar. Stir well and leave until the process of fermentation has settled down. Strain into carefully sterilized bottles. Although it can be drunk much sooner, it is best left for a year.

During the seventeenth century the number of Amerindians in Trinidad was halved to around 15,000. The remainder supplied the slave labour for the Spanish estates and pearl fisheries until as late as the 1780s. After that most of those sickened and died, often of the smallpox introduced by the colonizers. In Grenada they elected to commit mass suicide and leapt to their deaths at Sauters, a wild rocky part of the coastline thrashed constantly by the seas. The very few that remained interbred or, in the case of the island of Dominica, were put on reservations.

Today there are still reminders of the Amerindian and his style of eating and food preparations. For instance, the guava, an indigenous fruit tree, grew throughout the West Indies and the Indians ate its fruit raw. I was recently touring another plantation house that had been opened to the public, when the heady aroma of what I thought were tomato plants passed me in volatile mists, distilled from the plants outside in the old kitchen gardens. So overpowering was their perfume, I traced it to the kitchens, to find not tomatoes, but a fruit those same Indians taught us to eat; the guava, being stewed for our dessert. Here I found the cook was a local woman who happily explained to me that the fruit lends itself well to being made into jams, jellies, nectar and cheese.

Guava jelly is to be found throughout many of the islands and is sold at roadside stalls in varying shapes and sizes of medicine bottles, which have been carefully collected over the months.

She showed me that to make **Guava Jelly** you must peel the fruit first, then crush it, putting it into a large pot and covering it with cold water. This she brought to the boil and stewed until the fruit was quite soft, then strained, first through a colander and then through a piece of muslin or strong old cloth, allowing the juice to drip into a bowl. However much juice was extracted, she would measure and equal cup for cup of white sugar. The juice was then reheated to dissolve the sugar, without letting it boil. For each cup measured, she now added approximately half a teaspoon of freshly squeezed lime juice. Only then, she explained, did she bring it to the boil, skimming off the 'gum' with a large wooden spoon 'all the while'. The simple test she applied to see if it was jelling was to drop a little on a saucer. It might be necessary to put the saucer in the fridge for a minute or two to be sure. Allow to cool and bottle.

Today, if you travel to the Orinoco river on the South American mainland in Guyana, which is just a few miles across the straits from Trinidad, you will still find the Amerindian living much as he has always done, in his thatched hut near a manioc clearing.

OUR MEN ARE
PLANTING APACE

Then came the men with eyes as heavy
as anchors who sank without tombs

Derek Walcott

The Caribbean had been appearing on European maps of the world for over a hundred years when in 1627 Charles I made the Earl of Carlisle 'absolute lord of all the Caribbee islands lying between ten and twenty degrees north latitude'. Charles I explained that his grant of lordship to Carlisle, which overrode William Courteen's right, derived 'from a laudable and zealous care to increase the Christian religion'.

The real motivation, of course, was to seize the opportunity offered by the success of the first plantings of tobacco. News of the potential pickings had been reaching home ever since the arrival in Barbados of the first settlers and travellers, who sent back glowing reports of the richness of the rain forests and the abundance on sea and land of 'fish and fowle'. One account ran: 'The land lyeth high, much resembling England, more healthful than any of hir neighbors, and better agreeing with the temper of the English nation.'

Another visitor was Sir Henry Colt. He came from an English family with a tradition of adventuring. Some of them became pioneers in America and developed the firearm that was named after them. Henry Colt was the only member of his family, apart from a nephew, who travelled to the West Indies. He arrived four years after the first boatload of settlers and wrote of 'the marvellous swiftness of air and soil. As soon as the rains start and the soil is easily turned the corn and peas are planted and bear in three months.' He also noted fig trees, vines, oranges, lemons, plantains, pomegranates, Indian wheat – red and white – all of which apparently bore fruit after being in the ground for a very short time.

The English squirearchical tradition transplanted to the West Indies differed from that at home in one important way: in the West Indies, gentlemen possessed indentured labour. Richard Ligon recorded that the 'island is divided into three sorts of men, viz, masters, servants and slaves'. In the middle of the sixteenth century there were only some 800 slaves and, according to Ligon and other observers, they 'and their posterity being subject to their masters for ever' were preserved with greater care than the English servants 'who are theirs but five years'.

The masters included both the first settlers, who were treated as tenants by the companies who funded the civilization, and the planters or estate owners, whose rights were established by Carlisle's land grants. The tenants were not allowed to own land and had to return all their profits to London.

Some of the original settlers were the younger sons of English noblemen and well-positioned gentlemen farmers, who did not receive an inheritance. Others were the middle and lower orders of village and town – unemployed craftsmen, peasants, yeomen and farmer copy-holders, some of whom had been pushed out of their old secure franchise by rising rents, unemployment and increasing competition for land, into the position of leaseholders or tenants at will. The lure of the New World was the promise of a new start and free land.

At the top of the hierarchy some twenty or so families emerged, who later came to dominate the history and development of Barbados. Today much of their wealth has been dispersed, but their descendants often remain; known as 'High Whites', they still rank as the island elite and, in many cases, still own their old original plantation homes.

When a boat came in with fresh arrivals of servants from England, the planters would go on board and 'buy such of them as they liked'. They would then send them with a guide to the plantation, where they were instantly told to make their own cabin. If they knew not how, they spent the night on open ground until some other more experienced servant helped them. The dwelling was crude enough, and was made of sticks, vines and plantain leaves to keep the rain off and shade them from the sun. Their supper was invariably potatoes and bone meal twice a week. They worked their small plots with the help of one or two of the first shiploads of American slaves or indentured labourers.

The feelings of loss and separation of all these groups involved in opening up the New World appear, from their diaries and correspondence home, to have been traumatic and devastating. John Atkins, a ship's captain on the Royal Navy's ship *The Swallow*, was to write later, 'A man whose means of subsistence irreversibly depends on the sea is unhappy because he forsakes his wife, children, country and friends, all that can be called pleasant (and of necessity not choice) to tempt unknown dangers on that deceitful trackless path.' His journey took some eight months via West Africa. He wrote with great dramatic sense that as they sailed from England, the seas crashed on the rocks 'with terrible accent to lament the separation, who knows but we likewise severing ourselves eternally from our friends'.

For the new estate owners, the quality of life soon equalled that back home. In a short space of time, the planters had organized their new plantation homes to function just as their English country houses had done. If visitors had not written so much about the opulent standard of living, you might initially doubt whether it could really have taken place so far from home.

Richard Ligon, one of the first travellers to report back to us in detail, wrote of the 'victuals from different parts'. There was beef, brought from Holland, Old and New England, Virginia, and Russia – which 'yet comes to us sweet' – plus every kind of saltfish from ling and haberdine to cod and poor John. No estate was more than ten miles from the sea in any direction, and the plantation kitchens became renowned for their supplies of good fish such as 'Mullets, Parrot fish, Snapper, red and grey Corallos, Trebums, Crabs, Lobsters and Coney fish'.

As the earliest settlement flourished, more ships were sent from England in the 1630s and 1640s, with men, provisions and extra working tools to cut the woods and clear the ground to plant a greater variety of vegetables and fruit trees. By the end of the century an impressive range of fruits, vegetables and herbs had been successfully imported and planted; a reflection of the many new plants brought by explorers to Britain at this time and of changing attitudes. Vegetables were appearing more regularly on both poor and wealthy tables. Harrison, the Elizabethan historian, points this out in his *Description of England*. He wrote that herbs, fruits and roots that grow yearly out of the ground were much neglected until Henry VIII, but from then on their use was resumed 'not only among the poor, I mean of melons, popons [pumpkin], gourds, cabbage, radishes, parsnips, carrots, peas, cucumbers, and all kinds of salad herbs, but also fed upon as daintie a dishes at the tables of delicate merchants, gentlemen and the nobility, who make their provision yearly from the new seeds out of strange countries from whence they may have them abundantly'. English labourers grew vegetables on their own small plots of land and the country houses often had completely walled kitchen gardens for herbs, fruit and vegetables. By 1577 *The Gardener's Labyrinth*, the first gardening handbook, had already been published.

In the Caribbean the successful planting of new varieties owed much to the Amerindian, who carefully nurtured each crop, and even more to the richest soils in the world. Because many of the islands were volcanic (though in Barbados it was coral), you would often have to dig some three feet of soil to reach the 'tiff' or rock as they call it here. In the dry season the soil hardens and cannot be turned, but with the first rains in June and July it becomes moist and yielding and vegetables can be forked out easily.

English settlers were able to contribute some of their newly acquired experience, and bring varieties of fruits, vegetables and herbs to complement the New World's supply of squash, runner beans, tomatoes, avocados, capsicums, potatoes and sweet potatoes.

New fruit trees such as the tamarind were brought in from the East Indies. The pulp from the tamarind's seeds was used to form the basis of many sauces, including those we know today such as bottled Worcester, pepper and brown sauces. The settlers also made a wine from it by attaching a bottle under a cut made into the bark and draining the sap; it was said to be delicious, but it only kept for a day or so. Fig and cherry trees were less successful for their fruit was said to be insipid. The orange was also unsuccessful, although today they have engineered several very acceptable strains. Limes and avocados were brought from the mainland, and it was often noted by Europeans at the time that lime was much better than the lemon juice they were accustomed to in Europe. Imported pomegranates, lemons and citrons, claimed to be the parents of the lemon and lime from Europe, did well too. Ligon mentions the coconut, which supposes that it had arrived there by the middle of the seventeenth century. He said that he had carried his own seeds to grow herbs such as rosemary, thyme, marjoram, parsley, tarragon and sage, which all thrived there. He also carried with him garlic and the seeds for onions, marigolds, cabbage and turnips.

Life on the estates in the early days was by no means the set-piece affair that one might imagine. There was much toing and froing, usually by canoe, or boat – 'battoe' as they then were called – since the roads were often impassable because of the heavy rains. In remoter regions this is still the case today.

Extra labour was frequently sought and exchanged for the difficult transport of goods and provisions: slaves were lent wherever required and white supervisors and tradesmen, free and indentured, were involved in ever-changing enterprises. Sometimes each estate would supply its own labour when much needed work was to be done on the roads. This regular interchange of peoples naturally led to social intercourse and the pooling of ideas on planting, recipes and cures. Minced chicken guts, for example, became a cure-all for sick animals. The guts were minced or chopped, mixed with liquor and put in a horn to give to the animal. Few recovered and often, when they did, they had become so emaciated that they were useless for toil or consumption. The problem then was to find new animals in time to bring in the ripe cane harvest.

The planters' lives could be lonely at times and they would have been glad for the chance of each other's company and any excuse for a dinner party. These were invariably held whenever ships' captains, the militia and the like would pass through, bringing fresh accounts of the voyage and welcome news of home. Records suggest that awesome quantities of alcohol were consumed on such evenings, no doubt loosening the tongues of most men and encouraging the 'ole talk' to flow through the night. One Lieutenant Governor of the day, together with his dinner guests, disposed in one evening of six dozen bottles of claret at fifteen shillings each – these appear to have come from a French Privateer that had been seized and held captive in the Bay – three dozen bottles of hock at three pounds ten shillings, a dozen bottles of Spanish champagne at seventeen and six per bottle, four dozen bottles of Madeira wine and a further eight dozen ciders.

Good use of the ample supplies of wine and spirits was also made in the dishes for such occasions. Wild or Muscovy duck was often cooked in claret, and prepared in much the way as described below. The point of the rather elaborate procedure is that while the sauce is impressively rich in flavour, the duck is served separately and the flavour of the meat remains intact, so make sure that you choose a good fresh, preferably wild, duck.

To cook **Duck in Claret** you will need a good fresh duck for four people, which you then salt and marinade in white rum. Choose a well-flavoured white rum and rock salt: rub both well in and refrigerate for twenty-four hours only. Drain off and wipe thoroughly to dry the carcass. Rub the duck inside and out with plenty of olive oil, black pepper and crushed garlic, the juice of a lime and some salt, then place in an open roasting pan. The legs take much longer to cook than the breast, so you should turn the bird on to its side for thirty minutes and turn again for the other leg for another thirty minutes. This way the breast will be perfectly succulent and the legs properly cooked. This will take approximately one hour. Now put the duck under the grill to crisp the skin a little and turn it to a golden brown. Baste once or twice with the fat that the duck has produced while roasting. While the duck is cooking, prepare the sauce. You will need all the giblets, 600 ml (1 pint) of meat stock, 2 medium onions, 1 whole head of garlic with its skin left on but cut diagonally, 1 carrot, 3 tablespoons of parsley, 3 tablespoons of celery, 120 g (4 oz) of salt pork (from any Spanish or Italian importer), black pepper, salt if necessary to taste, 4 tablespoons of olive oil, 60 g (2 oz) of unsalted butter and 150 ml (¼ pint) of good claret. Chop the onions, celery and parsley as small as possible so they will melt away to a pulp as they cook. Slice the carrot very thinly too. Chop the salt pork and the bone if it is soft enough, or else leave it, into small cubes. Put the oil and butter together in a large frying pan on a moderate heat and fry all the ingredients. Heat the wine slowly, but do not let it boil, and when the vegetables have quite softened down add the wine. Bring it all to a fierce bubble for a few moments, then add half of the warmed stock, let it simmer and reduce for one hour. Strain the sauce and put in the fridge to bring the fat to the top; skim off gently. Sieve the vegetables and all the giblets except the neck. When you reheat the sauce, add as much as you like of the sieved vegetables and remaining stock to thicken the sauce to your taste. Try frying sliced cooked yams or sweet potatoes in the fat from the pan that the duck was cooked in, until they are crisp and golden on each side. I like to serve the dish sprinkled with fresh chopped parsley.

White rum is an ideal spirit to combine with local young chickens, flavoured delicately with a sprinkling of mace. Try this delicious stewed **Poussin in Rum.** For two people, allow one poussin cut in half lengthways, 25 g (1 oz) of unsalted butter, 2 tablespoons of olive oil, 50 g (2 oz) of salted pork, a pinch of freshly ground mace and black pepper, salt to taste, 1 tablespoon of white rum, ½ a medium onion – finely diced, a pinch of cayenne pepper and dried thyme, 1 tablespoon of tomato sauce and 50 ml (2 fl oz) of good thick cream. Heat the oil and butter in a heavy frying pan and gently fry the salted pork, which you have to cut up into very small pieces, for ten minutes. Add the chicken, onions, seasoning and rum. Cover with a well-fitting lid. Stew very gently until the meat comes away from the bone. Put the chicken halves to brown under the grill for a few moments. Add the tomato sauce and stir into the juices in the pan; now add a little boiling water to make the sauce to the thickness you would like, approximately 125 ml (4 fl oz), bring to the boil for a minute, then add the cream. Boil for another minute, stir very well to amalgamate all the bits and pieces from the chicken, salted pork and the juices. Take straight off the heat and serve by pouring over the chicken. There should be no need to add any salt since the salted pork should provide enough.

The menus and kitchen accounts for such dinners provide a good picture of the way in which English dishes were introduced to the plantation kitchens and adapted to local ingredients. Ligon visited all the great estates and left us with detailed descriptions of the dinners he enjoyed. At the table of Colonel James Drax, one of the fifty-nine who were granted settlements and whose descendants still live in both Barbados and England, he was served a great 'regalio' of beef. Pieces of boiled rump, roasted chine, breasts and tongue, were served alongside tripes in pies seasoned with sweet chopped herbs, suet and currants, leg pallets, olla podrida – a Spanish dish – and, finally, a dish of marrowbone.

This princely repast was followed with, 'potato pudding, a dish of Scots collops of a leg of pork, as good as any where in the world, a fricassee of the same, a dish of boiled chickens, a shoulder of young goat dressed with his blood and thyme, a kid with a pudding in his belly, a sucking pig, which there is fattest, whitest and sweetest in the world, with a poignant sauce of the brains, salt, sage and nutmeg done with claret wine, a shoulder of mutton, which there is a rare dish, a pastry of the side of a young goat and a side of fat young shot [a young hog three months old] upon it, well seasoned with pepper and salt and with some nutmeg, a loin of veal, to which their wants no sauce being so well furnished with oranges, lemons and limes, three young turkeys in a dish . . .' – and so the list continued.

Colonel Drax had not always been able to entertain in such a lavish style, for when he came to the island he had 'a stock not exceeding three hundred pounds stirling'. He raised his fortunes so greatly that people said they had heard him say he would not look to England until he was able to buy an estate which provided an income of at least £10,000. This he expected to accomplish, by all accounts, in just a few years from the profits made from planting sugar cane.

The evident generosity Ligon enjoyed at Drax's table was not exceptional, judging by the account books of other plantation houses. A popular recipe was the following opulent crabscoe of crawfish, which comes from a seventeenth-century folio manuscript belonging to a planter's family originally from Beaminster in Dorset. In the heavy rains of tropical storms, crawfish are washed down in great numbers into the bays and easily picked up. I particularly like the use of the pounded shells in this recipe.

 To make a **Crabscoe of Crawfish**, the writer of the recipe suggested collecting a hundred or more crawfish and, after taking out the tails, pounding the shells very fine and stewing them slowly in a pan, with a pound of good butter, over a low heat. The butter was then strained into another stew pan and left to get cold, then worked into a cream with a wooden ladle. By degrees, yolks of eggs, the crumbs of a French roll steeped in cream, a little nutmeg and lemon peel were added. Sugar, worked together with a little more cream, could be added for a sweet pie. A rim of pastry would be made round the edge of a dish, the egg and cream liaison and the crawfish tails put inside and the pie baked for half an hour. I adapt this, skipping the sugar and, of course, cutting the quantities.

A more modest dish that occurred frequently in menus and diaries was salamongundy, which was taken out to the West Indies from England in the early 1600s. Mrs Glasse, who in 1747 had described it as a large dish of separate ingredients that were minced and shredded, emphasized that 'you may always make Salamongundy of such things as you have according to your fancy'. This sensible dish became established throughout the West Indies, and today appears more frequently there than in England. Usually called herring gundy or gungry, the basic idea is that salted meats and fish are used to enliven the taste of any leftovers.

For **Herring Gundy** for four people you will need 500 g (1 lb) of salted herring soaked overnight, 500 g (1 lb) of cold cooked potatoes, 1 mild red onion, 2 grated carrots, 2 cooked and sliced beetroot, some chopped seasoning peppers, parsley, and 2 large, cold hard-boiled eggs. The herrings can be soaked in milk or water overnight. Then peel off the skin, remove the bones and chop up. The flesh will fall apart quite easily. Some people mash the herrings with the potatoes, but I prefer to chop all the ingredients quite coarsely, including any leftovers of cold meat from a joint of beef or lamb or roast chicken, and dress them with a vinaigrette of olive oil and wine vinegar. Grind fresh black pepper over it all. If salted herrings are not available, use a dozen or so anchovies. Chill before serving.

Salting was used extensively to preserve all meat and fish. Much of it was imported already salted, but it was also preserved in this way locally. I was given the following recipe for salted duck by an elderly man of African descent in Barbados, whose wife had 'long died'. Her salted duck, if nothing else, still stirred memories. He described how she had rubbed the duck liberally with salt and left it for three days, then washed it and roasted it plain. I could not imagine how this would be, so I decided to investigate and see if I could find any traces of such a dish for myself. Of course it was Elizabeth David who had come across one such method which she called Welsh salt duck. Was it taken to the West Indies by a group of Welsh people who came to Grenada many generations ago and have lived in isolation? Elizabeth David said that she had first found it in print in 1867. It is very well worth doing.

For **Salted Duck** you will need a duck large enough for four people. Rub it all over with 120 g (4 oz) of rock salt, which I put in the blender first. Then place in a deep dish in the refrigerator and cover. Once or twice a day for three days, rub the salt in again. The skin turns a strange white colour and the bird appears to shrink a little. Before cooking it wash off the excess liquid that has been produced, and the salt. Put the bird in an oven dish deep enough to hold it and cover it with cold water. Cook on a low heat (150°C, 310°F, Gas mark 2) for approximately two hours. Serve it cold with pickles and a green salad. The taste of the duck is remarkably good and unadulterated. The other advantage is that there will be almost no fat left on the duck.

Ligon wrote that pork was the best of the local meat available; great care was taken over the rearing of the sows, barrow hogs and boars – 'they are the sweetest flesh of that kind that I have ever tasted, and the loveliest to look on . . . when I came first to the island, I found the pork dress'd the plain wayes of boyling, roasting and sometimes baking in a dish.' When pigs were slaughtered in that heat, decisions would have to be made very quickly. What was not going to be eaten that day would be pickled and salted down. Ligon lamented turning it into bacon: 'It is very ill husbandry to practise it, for it must be cut in many places to let the salt in, and when it is dressed much goes to waste.'

Pigs are still reared in much the same way today, by individuals in their back yards and gardens. In the country areas, the slaughtering is usually done at a weekend; the squealing will direct you to the spot, where you will probably find the carcass already being cut up on the back of someone's truck. Fresh cuts can be marinaded safely in a cool place overnight for the temperature mostly drops to 24°C (75°F) or even less in the winter months. A typical recipe today is the following:

For **Barbecued Pork Chops** for four people you will need 4 thin loin chops marinaded in ½ teaspoon of fresh lime juice, 1 dessert-spoon of clear honey, black pepper, 4–5 drops of pepper sauce or tabasco, ½ teaspoon of red wine vinegar, 2 tablespoons of tomato sauce and 2 tablespoons of freshly chopped coriander leaves. Mix all these ingredients in a bowl except one tablespoon of the chopped coriander. Prepare a charcoal fire and when the coals are good and red, barbecue the chops for six minutes each side, basting with the marinade. Serve with the remainder of the chopped coriander on top. In some of the islands you can use chardon beni which is rather like coriander in taste. It looks a little like the dandelion leaf. Serve with cubes of steamed pumpkin.

When you buy a piece of pork locally, you often get pork bones thrown in; there is no argument about this – you take it or leave it. However, they can be put to very good use in this very simple pork dish flavoured with allspice.

For **Pork in Allspice** for four to six people you will need 750 g (1½ lbs) of meat from the shoulder or the belly where, as they say in the islands, the meat is sweeter. In addition, ask your butcher to give you 500 g (1 lb) or so of pork or veal bones, broken up, so the marrow comes out easily. Cover the bones with water and bring to the boil; simmer for forty-five minutes, skimming off intermittently.

Set aside. To cook and season the meat, you will need coconut oil to cover the bottom of the frying pan, roughly a tablespoon of brown sugar, a very finely-chopped large Spanish onion, 2 cloves of crushed garlic, 1 tablespoon of freshly ground allspice, 1 teaspoon of salt, black pepper, 1 teaspoon of dried or fresh thyme, 1 tablespoon of red wine vinegar and a 50 g (2 oz) packet of coconut cream. Cut the fat off the meat and cut into cubes. Fry the pork in sugar and oil until it is a beautiful golden brown; add the onions and crushed garlic and salt. Sweat for ten minutes or until the onions are quite soft. Now add the allspice and fry for another five minutes, then add the black pepper and the thyme and enough juice from the bones to cover the meat; simmer for fifteen minutes and add the wine vinegar. Simmer for a further five minutes. Finally add the coconut cream. Let it melt in, stir well and cook for one hour longer with a well-fitting lid. If the sauce should become too thick, add a little more of the stock.

Allspice is used in the following recipe as well and is sometimes known as pimento, which is indigenous to the West Indies. It is one of the most characteristic West Indian flavours. One traveller to the islands in the nineteenth century wrote: 'Flocks of wild parrots smaller than our domestic kind feed on the allspice berries. The tree stands with its white blossom like an apparition of beauty amidst the darker foliage.' The slightest breeze awakes the fragrance and when the leaves are bruised, they omit a powerful scent almost as strong as the spice itself. I use the leaves as an alternative to bay; the brown berries are easily ground in the coffee grinder. Elizabeth David says they were much used in cooking to give an aromatic scent to marinades, soused herrings, salt beef and pickled pork. You will perfume the room if you only use very good beef, cooking it in allspice and lacing it with lime juice at the end.

For **Spiced Beef** for four people you will need 500 g (1 lb) of beef cut into small cubes, 2 teaspoons of grated fresh ginger, 1 teaspoon of salt, 1 Spanish onion, 4 cloves of garlic minced, 50 ml (2 fl oz) of coconut or vegetable oil, 12 coarsely crushed allspice berries, 1 teaspoon each of ground black pepper and coriander seeds, 1 heaped tablespoon of curry powder, 50 ml (2 fl oz) of water and the juice of 1½ freshly squeezed limes. Put the beef into a bowl and rub in the grated ginger and salt; leave for half an hour. Fry the minced onion and garlic in the oil until melted. Add the spices and cook for five minutes over a moderate heat; they must not burn. Then add the meat. Raise the heat to moderately high for a few minutes, stirring it thoroughly while letting it brown. Cover with a very well-fitting lid and reduce the heat again; let it simmer and sweat out its juices for thirty minutes. When you see that the oil has separated, add half the amount of water given and be careful that nothing sticks to the bottom of the pot; stay with it from now on. Cook for another ten minutes – the oil will separate again – add the remainder of the water and stir well. Cook very slowly until the meat is tender. Stir in the lime juice and sugar five minutes before serving.

Puddings were of such excellence and variety that they also caught Mr Ligon's attention. He wrote, ''tis fit we consider what *quelque chose* there are to be found that may service out a table of viands, as there are to be had; which are eggs several ways, viz, poch'd, and laid upon sippets of bread, soaked in butter and juice of limes, and sugar, with plumpt currants strewed upon them.'

Try this **Sippet** in egg and honey when you have a white loaf of bread going spare. For four people take 4 thick slices of bread cut into 3 cm (1 inch) wide strips, 125 ml (4 fl oz) of milk, 1 egg, 2 tablespoons of unsalted butter, 50 ml (2 fl oz) of clear honey – it is important to use a clear, free-running honey, preferably from the Caribbean region – and 50 ml (2 fl oz) of rum. Place the bread slices in a shallow baking dish and cover with the milk. Let it soak in for a few minutes, then using a slotted spoon, drain well on a clean towel. Beat the egg and dip the bread in the mixture. Heat the butter in a heavy frying pan and sauté the bread slices until they are brown all over. In a separate pan, mix together the honey and the rum, stir well, then pour over the bread slices. Bake for approximately fifteen to twenty minutes in a preheated moderate oven. According to Ligon, the sippets were finished off with a sprinkling of ground mace, cinnamon and cloves, with a touch of salt – though these spices are too strong for my taste. Sippets are delicious served hot.

Some other, more elaborate, pudding recipes taken to the West Indies by the English settlers still survive and have been adapted to make use of local flavourings. One of these is floating island pudding made with guava jelly and rum, which Sir Henry Colt maintained was better made than any he had eaten in England.

To make **West Indian Floating Island** for four people you will need 3 eggs with the whites separated from the yolks, 500 ml (¾ pint) of good single cream, 50 g (2 oz) of white sugar, 1 teaspoon of vanilla and 3 tablespoons of guava jelly, which you should leave out in the sun or in a warm place to soften. For the final dressing you will need 6 tablespoons of double cream, 3 tablespoons of good Jamaican rum and 1 tablespoon of white sugar to taste. Put the egg yolks and sugar in the top of a double boiler away from the heat and beat until the mixture is light in texture and colour. The single cream should be scalded and poured over the eggs in a steady stream. Put water into the lower half of the boiler and cook over a very gentle heat. You must stir it until it thickens and on no account should the water be allowed to boil. Pour into a broad serving bowl, allow to cool, then add the vanilla. Beat the egg whites until they form peaks; carefully fold in the jelly and drop in large spoonfuls very lightly on to the custard to make the floating islands. Whip the double cream with the sugar. When it is quite stiff, add the rum and whip for a little longer to ensure that it is well mixed in. Spoon this mixture around the edge of the dish.

On first coming to the Caribbean islands I was given the ingredients for another pudding that is just as rich in its generous use of cream and eggs:

To make this **West Indian Pudding** for four people you will need 600 ml (1 pint) of good thick cream, 100–125 g (4 oz) of loaf or granulated sugar, 250 g (8 oz) of sponge cake, 8 eggs and 75 g (3 oz) of preserved green ginger. Bring the cream to boiling point and add the pounded sugar to sweeten. Crumble the sponge cake in a bowl and when the cream has cooled pour it over the sponge. Beat the eggs and when the cream has been soaked up by the sponge, pour them over the mixture. Butter a mould generously and line it carefully with very thinly cut slices of the ginger. Pour in the pudding, trying not to dislodge the ginger slices; the pudding should then be tied down and steamed or boiled for an hour and a half. It is served with the syrup from the jar of ginger – try adding a little rum to this first.

Those who were in better positions, such as overseers, were able to afford homes and offer hospitality. Travellers and friends alike would enjoy conversation and catching up both on news from home and gossip circling the estates. They would eat a little before noon, apparently enjoying 'pickled herring, bread and punch'. Pickled herrings and mackerel are still staples on the shelves today; I had always imagined that they were introduced much later solely to feed the slaves, until I found numerous references in seventeenth-century sources. Ligon, for example, mentioned a very traditional dish called soused mackerel. You can create a similar dish today using red fish, herring or snapper.

For **Soused Fish** you will need a fish large enough for four people, 2–3 cloves, 2 bay leaves, 1 teaspoon of salt, 250 ml (8 fl oz) of water, 2–4 peppercorns, a piece of red hot pepper and 250 ml (8 fl oz) of vinegar. The fish should be scaled and boned, then cut into fillets which are rolled up and down in the salt, placed in a baking dish and covered with all the other ingredients before baking in a moderate oven for forty-five minutes. Ligon's account said that providing onion, chive or tomato were not used, the dish – to be served cold – would keep for four to five days.

The lives of the indentured men and women who were building up the estates in the 'brightest jewels in His Majesty's crown', were a stark contrast to the luxury in which the planters lived. They were the ones who brewed and baked, churned and ground the meal, bred, fed and slew their cattle and sheep, brought up the pigeons and poultry at their own doors, shod the horses and sawed planks, forged and mended the rough iron work, ran the mill and the slaughter house, the blacksmith's, carpenter's and painter's shop, the maltings and brew-house, the woodyard, laundry and dairy. The work was nothing new, following the pattern of self-sufficiency laid down by the English country house, but with the tropical climate and workload produced by the shortage of labour, their days were filled with the effort to survive.

Life must have been appallingly hard. I doubt they even had time to look up except to wish the sun was on its way down. There were a few planters who looked after their servants reasonably well, but nonetheless their existence could be difficult in the extreme. Servants were obliged to begin their day with the bell of the overseer dinning in their ears at six each morning. They worked until the bell rang again at eleven, when a mess of loblolly was served, with something called bonasift, the meaning of which I have been unable to trace. At one, they returned to the fields and worked through the rest of the day – whether it was the dry or rainy season – until six at night, to return to the same meal and a drink called mobbie to wash it down. 'Truly,' wrote Ligon, 'I have seen such cruelty done there to servants as I did not think one Christian could have done to another.' However, he did refer to one planter he knew, who, seeing his servants wet through with the rain and the sweat, sent to England for 'gowns, such as poor people wear in Hospital' so that they might rest warmer at night after their toils.

Rebellions did occur on some plantations. Mr Constantine

Sylvester, an eminent planter, had his house and sugar-cane burnt to the ground by the 'mischief and wilfulness of the servants'; but it was the negroes who showed their devotion to him by trying to stamp out the fires with their bare feet. 'Their sufferings and daily complaining', wrote Ligon, spread throughout the island, and many were persuaded to join the plot to kill their masters. The plan to cut their masters' throats and to become freemen was not discovered until the day before the intended revolt. Eighteen of the leaders, men who had come to the Indies from villages all over England, were put to death by hanging. Visitors to the island said that, while they were all men of good descent, their chief fault was drinking to excess; hardly surprising given the hard labour, poor lodging and diet and taxes levied on every person on the plantation. Forty pounds of tobacco was demanded from each offender, and additional taxes were collected from those who 'killed pigeon, or sold beer'; non-payment meant prison.

These men were accustomed to rearing cattle, sheep and poultry. In the Caribbean today it is interesting to see the importance of keeping good livestock, not for selling, but for the maintenance of the family. Neighbours are quite unperturbed that we attract their fowl, perhaps because of our more unusual leftovers. The chickens come smartly across the road and down to our house at half-past seven every morning to begin the days grubbing. I had always hoped that one would eventually choose to lay close by and, finally, at the beginning of one rainy season, there was an obvious and loud display of interest in a neighbour's hen by an exceedingly handsome cock, whose comb vied in brilliance with the flaming blossoms windfallen on the ground from the flamboyants. Some time later, the hen began foolishly to make joyous and self satisfied clucks, so that we knew where she had laid her eggs. One day shortly afterwards, the heavens opened with such a torrential downpour that the hillsides of our valley appeared to heave under a weight of water that is hard to describe or imagine – suffice to say that the records of the early settlers describe rains which washed lead coffins out of their resting place in the ground and out to sea.

Hours later, when the rain had finished, we went to look for the eggs, hoping to find them washed further down the hill. Instead we found our hen, a collection of dulled water-logged feathers, still sitting tenaciously on her nest. For hours she had withstood the bubbling torrent which had collected all the other effluence on the hillside and boiled along beside our house and over her nest. Such devotion demands a new appreciation of the sadly underrated hen and her struggles to protect her eggs. Now I think of her, too, as a descendant of those taken across the Atlantic by the first settlers.

Once we were given a hen as a present. In the days leading up to the intended meal, we fed her on bits and pieces we thought would further improve her flavour. The morning came when we felt she had developed enough; but by then we had got to know each other. To make it easier for her, we soaked some bread in white rum and fed it to her. Since hens are greedy and fairly indiscriminating in what they eat, her wings were soon drooping loosely to the ground, and her eyelids were already rolling heavenward when she met her end.

The recipe below, for stewed hen with peppers, makes a simple but delicious dish. This is a very old recipe, originally served with ship's biscuit, which Sir Henry Colt recommended. He said that Barbadian peppers were the finest he had found anywhere and were good used in all broths – or brofs as they say now – 'to ensure warmth in the stomach and keep away the flux'. If I am making this in England, I always try to buy imported maize-fed French chickens, since I find they taste much closer to the descendants of those brought to the West Indies.

To make **Stewed Hen in Pepper Sauce** cut a bird weighing enough for four people into quarters the day before the dish is to be eaten, and rub into them 2 teaspoons of fresh lime juice, salt and black pepper and a crushed clove of garlic. Leave this marinading overnight. You will now need 50 g (2 oz) of unsalted butter, 2 tablespoons of olive oil, 1 chopped and de-seeded seasoning pepper, 2–3 sprigs of fresh thyme (or half a teaspoon of dried thyme), 2 tablespoons of chopped parsley, 1 garlic head cut diagonally, 2 tablespoons of well-chopped carrots, 2–4 bay or pimento leaves, 250 ml (10 fl oz) each of white rum, red wine, water or chicken stock if you have any. Heat the oil and the butter together, then fry the chicken pieces, giblets, seasoning pepper and thyme together, until they have turned a good brown colour. Add the chopped carrots, parsley, garlic and crushed bay or pimento leaves and fry for a further few minutes. Add the rum, wine and water and cook at a rolling pace for thirty minutes with a lid on; lower the heat and simmer for another forty minutes or until the meat is tender. Remove the meat and giblets. Let the liquid cool and skim off the fat. Reduce the liquid over a high heat by half, cool again and skim if necessary. Heat the chicken and gravy together and serve with chopped parsley sprinkled over the dish.

Baked Sweet Potatoes make a good accompaniment to the stewed hen. Choose ones that are the size of a good baking potato, allowing one per person. Scrub the skins well and bake for at least forty to fifty minutes, then test as you would an ordinary potato to see that it is soft. Cut it in half and carefully remove the flesh and mash with unsalted butter and a little evaporated milk or single or sour cream; add some salt and black pepper to taste. Put through a sieve and put back in the casings.

I used the following **Chicken Stock** for the hen stew, but it can be used to great effect wherever a recipe calls for chicken stock. You will need one poussin or half a chicken, 100–125 g (4 oz) of salt beef, oil for frying, half a stick of celery, 1 tomato, 2 cloves of garlic, half a large onion, 750 ml (1¼ pints) of water, black pepper, 1 seasoning pepper and 2 sprigs of thyme. Cut the salt beef into very thin slices against the grain and fry in the oil for about fifteen minutes; add the chicken which should be roughly chopped up into small pieces and turn for a few minutes, then chop roughly all the remaining ingredients and add to the pot; cover with water and cook gently for an hour. Strain, cool and skim. Keep the strained liquid for the hen stew recipe or freeze.

A simple way that the early settlers or indentured people used for cooking poultry or wild game was to season it and put it straight over the hot coals. Even now, when we prepare rather more elaborate meals for our barbecue, locals think nothing of putting a whole chicken – or squid or octopus – straight over the coals. There is no preparation at all, save for washing it in the sea water. It is usually eaten with no seasoning of any kind. It is just as good, if not better.

In an itinerary written by Fynes Moryson in 1670, it was observed that, 'in the seasons of the year the English eat fallow deer in plentifully . . . which they bake into pasties'; this he went on to say was considered a 'dainty rarely found in any other kingdom'. That especially English taste for pasties was introduced to the West Indies and has remained a popular and everyday lunch time snack for many people, but today they use minced or ground beef. I found the following method for making it, by Barbara Kopytoff, in *The Anthropologist's Cookbook*.

For **Jamaica Pattie** you will need 375 g (12 oz) of self raising flour, 1 teaspoon of salt, 250 g (8 oz) of butter, 350 ml (12 fl oz) of cold water and 1 teaspoon of paprika to make the pattie case. Put all the above in a large enough bowl to mix and add approximately a third of the water or enough to make a soft dough. Knead gently and set aside in a cool place. For the filling you will need to cook 1 kg (2 lbs) of ground beef,

2 cups of breadcrumbs, 1 teaspoon of very finely chopped hot red pepper, 1 medium onion very finely diced, 2 cloves of crushed garlic, a few leaves of fresh thyme, salt to taste and 250 ml (8 fl oz) of hot water. Fry the beef in a pan very gently, letting the fat run off and which you should then strain. Add the other ingredients and the boiling water. Cook for another fifteen minutes. I would mince or blend the ingredients with the water and mix the paste into the ground beef and cook it for the same length of time. Taste to adjust your seasonings, then roll out the pastry very thinly to ½ cm (⅛ inch) in thickness, cut in small rounds and put some filling on one half of the pastry. Fold and press edges with a fork to seal. Brush with a little oil, which the Jamaicans sometimes colour reddish with annatto, and bake for approximately twenty-five minutes at 180°C (350°F, Gas mark 4).

The annatto tree is native to the West Indies and, although I have seen it growing in other islands, its use as a colouring and flavouring is particularly favoured in Jamaica. It is the orange pulp surrounding the seed that is used for colouring and flavour, though I have ground the seeds themselves and fried them in the oil first before beginning to cook the dish; this also colours and flavours a little.

Brawn – usually known in the West Indies as souse – was another cheap source of food for the poorer folk in Barbados, but its popularity later spread throughout the islands. Today the head is still relished and to the extent that, since there are not so many animals available for slaughter at any one time, orders have to be put in with the butcher to be sure of getting one. I have been rather taken aback in the past to see a car boot open at the side of the road and to find myself looking down into the calm face of a cow or bull.

As Elizabeth David points out in her recipe for a pork or pig's head cheese – a close relation to the West Indian souse – 'salting gives it a better flavour and the saltpetre a better colour'. The sousing and brining of meat and fish was an everyday necessity in order to keep it longer in the heat. Such was the emphasis on good salt and sugar that, where the household could afford it, the best quality was always bought. In the West Indies in the nineteenth century it was recognized that the best sugar to be used was known as 'foots of sugar', for it was double in strength and was to be found at the bottom of every cask of West Indian sugar when it was first opened.

To prepare **Beef in Brine,** Elizabeth David quotes Florence Jack's method. You will need 750 g (1½ lbs) of sea salt (bay salt) or failing that, common kitchen salt, 200 g (7 oz) of brown sugar, 30 g (1 oz) of saltpetre and 5 litres (1 gallon) of water. All these ingredients should be brought to the boil and continued on the boil for another fifteen minutes, skimming all the while. She said that pickling is best done in cool weather so in the West Indies we begin at nightfall when the temperature drops deliciously. Use an earthenware crock with a well-fitting wooden lid, if possible. Strain the liquid when it has cooled and pour into the crock, then add the meat. She says it must be completely immersed and turned every day. I would continue this for possibly eight to ten days. The meat should come away from the bone easily. Remove the skin and gristle from around the ear, snout and tongue. Chop all the meat and slice the tongue. Taste for more salt. The meat will need highly seasoning with black pepper, finely chopped seasoning peppers, perhaps one carefully de-seeded hot pepper and at least all the juice from a fresh lime or it will be insipid and cloying.

If you arrive in time for the slaughter ask for some liver too, for it is very good if prepared in the following way.

For **Liver Marinaded in Lime Juice** for four people you will need 450 g (1 lb) of calves' or pigs' liver, the juice of 1 large lime, black pepper, 2 tablespoons seasoning, 250 ml (8 fl oz) of chicken stock, 1 medium onion, 1 tablespoon each of finely chopped celery, carrot and parsley, 4 chopped cloves of garlic, coconut oil to fry, 1 tablespoon of tomato sauce, 4 tablespoons of cooked pumpkin and salt to taste. Partially freeze the liver so that it is then easier to cut into ½ cm (⅛ inch) thick slices. Marinade for one hour in the lime juice and black pepper, then mix in the seasoning and leave for another hour. Fry the celery, carrot, parsley, garlic and onion in the coconut oil until they are soft. Bring the stock to the boil and add the fried vegetable, drained of any remaining oil. Remove any juices from the liver, pat it dry and fry it in the oil for a couple of minutes each side; add to the stock with the tomato sauce. Blend the boiled pumpkin and stir into the sauce. If it is reluctant to blend without some liquid, add a little of the chicken stock. Simmer for thirty minutes and serve with plain boiled rice and pumpkin.

The 1640s were pivotal years for the British plantations in the Caribbean. On the one hand, the Civil War brought political upheaval and in its wake, Cromwell's 'Western Design'; on the other, the planters were re-tooling and turning their plantations over from tobacco to sugar-cane, which marked a period of unprecedented prosperity. The days of the small plantation owners were fast disappearing and making way for the big sugar producers. The quest for the production of the 'white gold' was under way.

Large numbers of extreme Royalists began to settle in Barbados, holding the balance of power and giving rise to fears in England that the Civil War would be continued and fought from there. 'Reduce Barbados to the obedience of the Commonwealth,' went the warrant issued by Sir George Ayescu, which gave orders to 'force the inhabitants to submission, surprise their forts . . . beat down their castles and places of strength and to seize all ships and vessels belonging to them or any other trading there.'

Influential planters' fears that trade would be badly hit by the blockade, won considerable numbers over to the Commonwealth side and the power switched to the Republican elite. Now, with Barbados secure and with the political backing, the rich resources of the plantation owners and the conscripts from the labourers to hand, Cromwell launched his grand 'Western Design' – his reprisal against the almost complete Spanish domination of the whole Caribbean. The change in the balance of power was to last until the present day. Jamaica, which alone had twenty-six times more land available for planting, was seized by the British, as were the smaller islands of Nevis, St Kitts, Montserrat and Antigua, and swift economic changes followed in the islands.

So fast was the development of the new sugar estates in the islands taken by the British that one seventeenth-century writer observed that ships had transported from them as many goods in ten years, as the Spanish did out of the empires of Peru, Mexico, Hispaniola and Jamaica put together. In London the proceeds of the sugar trade were transformed into trading houses, banks and state banks and made the fortunes of certain powerful families. These activities and the fact that the estates were largely managed from England enabled the investments to be mainly ploughed back into the English economy. But enough wealth was kept in the islands to ensure that the great houses became grander than ever. They now stood in the centre of a landscape that was changing dramatically. Next to the great house sprang up the stone sugar mills, their great rotating arms dominating the skyline; close by were the boiling houses and slave baraccons, then built of mud and wattle. Beyond, every suitable piece of land was criss-crossed by lines of cane sticks and bent figures tending them during their precious growth.

Throughout the West Indian islands today you can still find many of the buildings in ruins, the mills only standing through the support and embrace of the trees and vines that have taken root in the cracks in the lime and mortar. However, a number of them are still working. In Grenada they are being restored and the sugar factories cannot get enough cane to crush for their needs. High above St Georges an old stone sugar factory, built in 1800, sits atop a ridge, catching the trade winds and affording stunning views of the Atlantic and Caribbean seas as you look from east to west. Far below spread valleys, planted with sugar-cane just ripening. To step inside the building is to marvel that the scene has changed so little. The only major change is that the cane is no longer crushed by the laborious physical treading of the wheel, which the slaves once powered with their legs like rats set to work in a cage. Since the arrival of the Industrial Revolution, the great iron wheels have been turned by water, brought down from high in the mountains by stone viaducts.

But everything else is done by hand, as it has always been. Underneath, the brick chimneys still carry fires, fuelled by the newly dried crushed cane grass, through ducts under the coppers. As it matures, the liquid is ladled from one copper to another with the same long wooden stick, an old iron pot tied to the end where there once would have been a crucible. The drums are filled with the rich molasses and, once cool, they will fill your bottle for you if you ask. Take the molasses home and make a traditional West Indian dark cake with it.

You will have to prepare the fruit for a **Dark Cake** two to three weeks in advance by buying 1.1 kg (2¼ lbs) of mixed fruits such as 120 g (4 oz) of raisins, 300 g (10 oz) of sultanas, 250 g (8 oz) of currants, 250 g (8 oz) of prunes or dates, 100 g (3½ oz) of mixed peel, and 100 g (3½ oz) of cherries. You may arrange the quantities as you like, but I would only use 120 g (4 oz) of cherries. Wash and dry very carefully, removing all the water. Then put in a large jar and cover with dark rum. Some people mince the fruit before soaking, which gives a marvellous and unusual texture. To make the cake once the fruit is soaked, beat together 250 g (8 oz) each of white sugar and unsalted butter until really creamy and without a hint of any grains of sugar. Now slowly add 6 very well-beaten large eggs, stirring vigorously to avoid curdling. Carefully fold in 250 g (8 oz) of white flour, 2 teaspoons each of ground allspice and cinnamon, three quarters of a teaspoon of ground mace and half a teaspoon of nutmeg (which is much better if it is freshly ground just before you use it). Now stir in 125–150 ml (4 fl oz) of the molasses or West Indian dark treacle, and half a teaspoon of vanilla and an eighth of a teaspoon of soda dissolved in a little warm water. Drain and dry the fruit thoroughly and stir into the mixture. See that it is all well-mixed in. Line your baking tin with heavy foil and pour in the cake mixture to within 3 cm of the top of the tin. Cook in a slow oven for at least three hours at 135°C (275°F, Gas mark 1). When done, prick the cake all over and pour 125–150 ml (4 fl oz) each of fresh dark rum and the juice that the fruit has soaked in all over the cake. If you are going to leave the cake for a few weeks, so much the better; at any time you can add a little more rum and it goes on improving. It keeps well in the fridge and is delicious sliced thinly and served very chilled.

Another by-product from the cane was sugar-cane brandy, which is a superb alcohol in which to cook the rather tougher meats over a long period. Even today in the Caribbean very little care is taken to see that the animals get shelter from the sun or the heavy rains and they must endure whatever the climate has to offer them. When you prepare to cook meat, except pork which is excellent, you have to accept that a lengthy preparation and cooking time get the best results.

Shoulder of lamb is excellent when cooked with a mixture of sugar-cane brandy and angostura bitters. The production of 'bitters' is now done in Trinidad and the recipe has always been a closely guarded secret. It was a Prussian army surgeon who travelled in 1820 to Angostura on the Orinoco river and discovered (I dare say from the Amerindians) a mixture of herbs and spices that became in demand throughout the world. It has long been used as a stomachic or stimulus for the appetite, and today is used to enhance rum based drinks, fruit cocktails, soups and the following stew.

 To cook **Lamb in Sugar-Cane Brandy**, or any good brandy, you must buy a fresh shoulder of lamb for four people and a pig's trotter. Skin and remove any thick areas of fat and cut the pig's foot in half. Rub the shoulder of lamb well with a marinade of olive oil, 4 cloves of crushed garlic and 2 tablespoons of good red wine vinegar, and lots of black pepper. Leave in a cool place overnight. Then assemble 50 ml (2 fl oz) of good extra virgin olive oil, 75 g (3 oz) of unsalted butter, 2 tablespoons of parsley, 1 whole head of garlic, half a stick of celery, 175 g (6 oz) of carrots, 1 large mild red onion, salt and black pepper to taste, 2–3 drops of angostura bitters, 50 ml (2 fl oz) of good quality sugar-cane brandy, 500 ml (¾ pint) of red wine and half a teaspoon of freshly ground allspice. Wash the trotter carefully

in water and lime juice. Heat the oil and butter together and brown the shoulder and trotter a little. Chop all the vegetables finely and the garlic head in half, removing any obviously loose skin. Add these and 1 tablespoon of the parsley, with the black pepper and salt to taste, and the angostura bitters. Simmer for an hour over a moderate heat keeping a lid firmly on. It is important to spend time checking to see that nothing is sticking. Add the sugar-cane brandy and wine; simmer for another hour. Serve the shoulder separately with the remainder of the parsley strewn over it and the freshly ground allspice. Strain the sauce and the trotter and serve separately.

Yet another of the by-products of the sugar-cane was kill-devil liquor, sometimes also called rumbullion, which was said to be an old Devonish word for rumbustious drunken behaviour brought here by the Royalist escapees from the Civil War. This was the drink in which the indentured labourers often sought solace. However, because by now there were people of several persuasions in Barbados, it was generally accepted that no matter how intoxicated they became, the words Roundhead or Cavalier should not be mentioned. The penalties were to give a shot or a turkey as an apology.

Kill-devil was a lethal drink when taken to excess and was distilled from the liquid skimmings of the coppers used to boil the sugar. It was then channelled off to the still-house and left to turn sour. Ligon recorded that the 'first spirit to be drawn off was called low-low wine, which was put into a still and drawn off again.' By now it was so strong that 'a candle being brought to a near distance to the bung of the hogs head or butt where it was kept, the spirits will fly to it, and taking hold of it, bring a fire down into the vessel and become a flame, breaking it and burning all about it.' One poor negro died in this way; he unwittingly brought a candle too near to see the better as he poured the liquid through a funnel, and was instantly transformed into a human torch.

A dram of this spirit was prescribed by the estate apothecaries to the negroes who were suffering from colds or sickness and sometimes to 'Christian servants' when their spirits were exhausted by hard labour and sweating in the sun for ten unimaginable hours a day.

A better use for strong spirits is to preserve what fruits are in season at the time in rum. The rum both conserves and imparts a delicious flavour. In the nineteenth century the rumpot method became very popular in Germany. I made it in Grenada with tropical fruits of my choice.

For a **Grenada Rumpot** choose a large jar which must be exceedingly clean and a very good bottle of dark rum. On the whole I find it unnecessary to peel any of the fruit. As each fruit comes into season, add to the pot and be sure that there are no blemishes on the fruit you choose. Wash it and dry it well and score gently into the fruit through the skin. Sprinkle with good brown sugar and leave for one hour; then put it into the jar and cover with the rum. Seal the top – clingfilm will seal it well enough – and keep stored in a dark cool place. I would advise you not to use any watery fruits that may dilute the rum, such as melon, apples and rhubarb, and to avoid sharp-tasting berries like gooseberries. Serve with a side dish of *crème fraiche* with a little rum and white sugar mixed in to taste. It is delicious.

With the continued and growing demand for indentured labourers, sources in England began to dry up. Replacements had to be found and the lower the cost, the better. In the years of political unrest between the Civil War and the Monmouth Rebellion in 1685, some 12,000 prisoners of war or political rebels, such as those for the Penrud Dock Rising or Rye House Plot, were transported to help solve the labour shortage. Convicts from English prisons such as Newgate were also shipped out, and the iniquitous practice of kidnapping young men off the streets was kept at full swing until 1682 when the Lord Chief Justice heavily fined the leading kidnapper and many of the remaining offenders threatened their customers – the colonial merchants – with the prospect of blackmail or turning informant.

Ireland was another considerable source of indentured labour. Under the old voluntary system, men and women paid for their shipping expenses by agreeing to captains selling their labour to the estates for periods of four to seven years. They formed up to a quarter of the population in islands such as Nevis. Later, Cromwell developed a plan to export a thousand Irish boys and girls, but there is no evidence to support whether or not this was carried out. We do know, however, that the governors of the various Irish counties were instructed to gather up vagrants from towns and countryside, whether they were men, women or children, and these were transported. To be 'Barbadosed' was an expression used at the time for anyone that was coerced one way or another and shipped out to the colonies. They were transported in the hold below deck throughout the long voyage and were not allowed on deck; twenty percent were thrown to the sharks.

The planters generally did not care for Irish labourers, considering them to be bad servants. Their fears of disloyalty were realized when the Irish in St Kitts defected to the French army. The remaining Irish throughout the other Leeward Islands were disarmed. Only Irish Town in Jamaica and Irish potatoes serve as their memorial today.

Forty years later, the Monmouth Rebellion produced another influx of labour. In the archives of Dorchester and Bridport, amongst others in the West Country, are sad lists of the names of prisoners taken at the Battle of Sedgemoor. The reprisals were terrible: the road from the battle site to Bridgwater was lined with men hanged on the gallows. Planters and speculators who held the greatest interest at Court immediately saw the opportunity for more cheap labour and received large consignments of prisoners. These prisoners who had not yet been hanged, found themselves sold for £10 to £15 apiece to the plantations.

The lists of names reveal that these men were from very different walks of life. One was a yeoman from Axminster, wounded at Sedgemoor, imprisoned, then transported on the good ship John from Weymouth to Barbados. Another poor soul was a Quaker who had been at the battlefield tending to the wounded on both sides. He had been caught on his way home, imprisoned, sentenced to death, then reprieved, and finally, despite the payment of ransom money by his family, shipped out to Barbados and sold to a Robert Bishop.

Today it is said that jug-jug, one of the most famous West Indian dishes to have been handed down through the generations, was first brought here by the Scots who were exiled after the Monmouth Rebellion. It seems quite believable to me since jug-jug bears an uncanny resemblance to haggis, with Guinea corn substituted for Scots cereal oats. In any case it is very good on a dark, warm, tropical night, especially accompanied by a whisky, in memory of the hundreds of Scots forcibly exiled to the islands.

 For **Jug-Jug** for four people you will need 175 g (6 oz) of salted beef brisket, 100–125 g (4 oz) of pickled pig's tail, 1 skinned chicken leg, 500 g (1 lb) of fresh pigeon peas (or canned if fresh are not available) 4 crushed garlic cloves, 2 medium onions, 2–3 sprigs of fresh thyme, 1 tablespoon each of finely chopped celery and parsley, 2 chopped seasoning peppers, 2–3 tablespoons of coconut or vegetable oil, black pepper, 50 g (2 oz) of finely ground corn meal, 500 ml (¾ pint) of coconut milk and 50 g (2 oz) of unsalted butter. Put the meats into enough water to cover, and simmer for an hour or until

the meat, especially the beef, is soft and easily shredded. Cool, strain, remove all the bones and shred the meat very finely. In another pan, cover the pigeon peas with cold water, bring to the boil and simmer until soft; this should take twenty minutes for fresh peas. Otherwise use canned peas; these are already cooked, so just drain them when ready to mash them. Chop the garlic, onions, thyme, celery, parsley and the de-seeded seasoning peppers as finely as possible, so that they look minced, and fry in a little oil for a few minutes until they are soft. Stir in the finely shredded meats and season with black pepper. Leave to one side for the flavours to blend while you put the corn meal in a pan. Add a little of the coconut milk to make a paste, put over a low heat and cook gently, adding 25 g (1 oz) of butter and the remaining milk a little at a time, stirring constantly so that the mixture does not stick. Cook in this way for fifteen to twenty minutes. Mash the peas on a large board with a rolling pin and stir in the corn meal, meats and seasonings. Mix carefully until amalgamated. Butter a bowl with the remaining butter, press the pudding mixture down firmly into the mould, then turn out and serve by cutting into slices.

But those temporary influxes of labour could not keep pace with the speed of development. It was a dramatic change indeed. The destruction of the countryside was so widespread and injudicious that there was no fuel to 'boyle their sugar' and they were forced to send to 'England for their coales'. More labour still was needed to clear large areas of woodland and plough them ready for the cane shoots. Finally, since the English could provide neither the much needed labour nor the skills to cultivate the cane, they were obliged to turn to the Dutch, who had begun to dominate Caribbean and European trade, buying up the sugar at good prices and trading in slaves from the West African coast. They were also willing to help with financial investment too. By the late 1650s, in Barbados alone, the numbers of Africans swelled from 5,500 to over 60,000. Over the next hundred years, what had begun as a mere trickle was to rise to a torrent.

For a while, the 'poor whites' or 'red legs' as they became known, performed the role of the militia to stand over the new African labour force. But many took to drink and the lives of the majority, it was said, became useless and dissolute. Forced sideways by the growth of slavery, large numbers of the whites slid to the bottom of the pile, into an almost forgotten and unwanted peasantry. Some moved to other islands, such as St Vincent or Bequia, and took to the sea for a living. A few went to Grenada and managed eventually to buy their own boats, putting down lobster pots, catching crabs, conch and a variety of fish. In Barbados today, their fishing skills are legendary.

Others remained in Barbados living as sharecroppers. By the time of emancipation in 1838, they did not seem capable of competing with the more newly acquired skills of the freed slaves and their situation worsened. Numbers dwindled through hardship and inbreeding until today when there are only some two hundred left, grouped together and mostly living in poverty in St Johns. Some were resettled in St Vincent where they lived and worked much as the slaves did before them, planting corn, cassava, ground nuts and today can still be seen cutting the sugar-cane.

Occasionally you still meet descendants of those early white labourers who came dreaming of free land and were left in poverty. On one of those rare nights in the Caribbean when the wind falls quite away and the sea is uncharacteristically still, a man with a curiously pale face and hair came and leaned on the door frame of the wooden rum shop. He began to speak with regret at not having planned to fish on such a night as this. It seemed to fill him with intense pain that the sea was holding her secrets in her depths without him. Where had his ancestors come from? He was not too sure, but the bleached hints of red in his head seemed to support something he had been told by his grandmother who had been told by her own grandmother that 'King James had something to do wid it'.

THE FOREMOST MEN
IN THE WORLD

Where are your monuments, your battles, martyrs?
Where is your tribal memory? Sirs
in that grey vault. The Sea. The Sea
The sea has locked them up. The sea is History.

Derek Walcott

The Jamaican countryside today looks much as it did in the eighteenth century, when it was the most productive of the sugar islands. It has by far the grandest of scenery and the most powerful mixture of different cultures in the Caribbean. Inland, the rugged wildness and beauty are staggering. The giant turkey buzzard cruises high above the uppermost ranges of the Blue Mountain peaks, which form the island's backbone. The roads, far below his curious and vigilant eye, outline the tops of the perilously narrow ridges. From here, there are overwhelming views on all sides: one looks down into the impossibly deep azure of the ocean or across rustic vales that are as heavenly green as England. Ghostly ruins of great houses, from where sugar empires were once ruled, rise from their well-chosen promontories. Far away, thin dust-red roads loop through the mountain jungle, basking in the deepening blue light.

Here you will find a way of life still very much undisturbed. You may quench your thirst at roadside stalls from green coconuts; a skilled man with a cutlash will take off the top in a few clean, if unnerving, strokes, so that you may drink the cool sweet water. Such was the fear of cholera that until recently those who could afford it, would lace it with a little brandy. To satisfy hunger you can buy a slice of yam roasted on charcoal and served with butter melting on it.

Yet for all this, Jamaica is an island as English in feel as Barbados. The country names resound with the planters' nostalgia for home: Cornwall, Westmorland and Surrey. Here the planters built homes on the grandest scale, trumping the style of living they had been accustomed to in England, naming the estates after Chatsworth, Vale Royal, Marlborough, Windsor and Kennilworth.

The wealth made from the sugar industry supported a lifestyle of incomparable opulence. 'As rich as a West Indian planter' became a common expression to describe anybody of great means. Materials were shipped into Jamaica along with the skilled craftsmen. Buildings of beautiful classic Georgian proportions were enhanced by Palladian windows, decorated on each side by wooden shutters or jalousies – elegant wooden fretwork decorating the spacious verandahs – which looked out over shaded parklands. Fine wrought-iron gates, brought from the English foundries, opened on to the sweeping drives which led up to the Great House.

Behind the Great House were the slave quarters or barracoons. Here the African, caught and enslaved by every possible deceitful ploy, settled in the Caribbean with only his 'tribal memory'. It is not known how many Africans were enslaved, but approximately 15,000,000 were sent to the Americas, of which at least 2,000,000 were taken to the British West Indian islands. A more lonely life would be hard to imagine. Deliberately separated from family, village and tribe, they were forbidden to speak their own tongues, or to play their own musical instruments. There was neither the time nor the scope on the estates to continue developing their own skills or practise their customs.

Who were these African peoples, taken in their millions from the so-called dark continent to the western hemisphere? Our understanding of their civilizations was destroyed by the European slave trade. As equality was superseded by slavery, which encroached ever deeper inland, and African enslaved African, so those who had any contact with the slave trade or the running of the estates to which they were sent, rationalized enslavement by arguing that Africa had no civilization and knew nothing of arts and science.

This view has pretty much prevailed until the last thirty years. It became impossible for the Europeans to accept that the men, women and children they had subjugated could have any sort of gifts, culture or intelligence. Indeed, the very lack of evidence after their subjugation naturally condemned them. The traditions of oral history, which in Africa had been recounted through many generations with perfect recall, could not withstand such a massive upheaval. Fortunately for us today, there were some people interested enough at the time to take down accounts of some of the slaves' personal experiences. One such account was given by Gustavus Vassa, an African who was enslaved and shipped to the West Indies. Gustavus's memory of his way of life in the homelands, the ordeal of the Middle Passage and adjustment to the New World makes for remarkable reading. He described his birthplace as a fruitful vale, and continued:

> It must have been a considerable distance from the capital of Benin and the coast, because I never heard of white men or Europeans, nor the sea, and our subjugation to the King of Benin was nominal. Our lands are uncommonly rich and fruitful, agriculture is our chief employment and everyone even to women and children are employed in it. Thus we are habituated to labour from our earliest years. Everyone contributes something to the common stock . . . Our tillage is exercised in a large plain or common, some hours walk from our village, and all the neighbours walk hither in a body. They use no beast of husbandry and their only instruments are hoes, axes, shovels and beaks or pointed iron to dig with.

All this knowledge and experience the Africans brought with them across the Atlantic. As the Brazilian sociologist, Gilberto Freyre, wrote, the African was 'the white man's greatest and most plastic collaborator in the task of agrarian colonisation in the Western Hemisphere'.

European accounts also give us a fascinating insight into the confidence of the African before his disruption. Leo Frobenius, the German historian, makes it clear in his history of the African civilization that the navigators of the fifteenth to the seventeenth century, mainly Portuguese, left strong proof of a black Africa which was in full efflorescence, harmonious and well informed:

> When they arrived in the Gulf of Guinea and landed at Vaida, the Captains were astonished to find streets well cared for, bordered for several leagues in length by two rows of trees, for many days they passed through a country of magnificent fields, a country inhabited by men and women clad in brilliant costume . . . to the South of the Kingdom of the Congo, a swarming crowd dressed in silk and velvet; great states, well ordered, powerful sovereigns, rich industries, civilised to the marrow of their bones . . . the conditions on the East coast were quite the same.

One of the few original accounts to survive the eighteenth-century earthquake which destroyed Lisbon, ran: 'With nauseating presumption these men will think themselves the foremost men in the world, and nothing will persuade them to the contrary. Never having been outside Africa, they imagine that Africa is not only the greatest part of the world, but also the most agreeable.' Similar opinions were held by the King himself, but in a manner still more remarkable: 'For he is persuaded that there is no other monarch in the world who is his equal, or exceeds his power or abundance of wealth.' Indeed at first the King of Portugal and the King of the Congo addressed each other as 'my Royal Brother'.

Earlier visitors from the Islam world left an equally clear picture of flourishing civilization. In 1352 Ibn Battuta wrote, 'One has the impression that the Mandingo state whose organisation and civilization could be compared with those of the Musselman Kingdoms or in Christian Kingdoms of the same epoch.' Later into the fourteenth century, Ramusio, Secretary to the Doge of Venice, instructed the Italian merchants to 'do business with the King of Timbucktu and Mali', for then it was a great city of learning and scholarship. Leo Africanus, the converted Moor and great traveller and writer, wrote after his return from the Songhay Empire, 'It is a wonder to see what plenty of merchandise is daily brought hither, and how costly and sumptious all these things be.'

This is the world from which the African came. The lands he left behind were by no means uniform in climate: between the northern desert zones and the rich tropical forests of the south there were dramatic contrasts. According to Gustavus, the West Indian plantocracy preferred their slaves to come from Ebo and Benin and not far from Guinea 'for their superiority and intelligence'. But the consensus of 1750, in which each slave was recorded by his tribe, shows the range of cultures: there were Kromatins, Ibos, Mandingoes, Mokos, Temne and Chamba.

But certain things could not be taken away. One was the African's deeply ingrained knowledge of agriculture, which developed long before European contact. Recently the idea that the impact of Islam was responsible for this development in the Sudan and West Africa has been refuted, and it is now being suggested instead that even the forest regions had their own indigenous methods of husbandry and domestication of food plants. From archaeological evidence and the increasing wealth of research given to us by a number of translations from Arab manuscripts that were written between the eighth and fifteenth century, it would seem that local varieties of millet and yams had been domesticated from species that grew wild, either in the Savannah or in the border country between the Savannah in the north and tropical forests in the south.

Rice and beans also played an important part in the grain foods of the people of West Africa, particularly in the Sudanic zone. There was a rice of indigenous origin, *Oryza barthii*, from which was cultivated *O. glaberrima*, and as early as 1300 Al Maghribi recorded that 'honey, butter and rice were very cheap'. Even earlier, in the tenth century, the Arab geographer, Ibn al Faqih, noted that kidney beans were part of the diet in the land of Ghana.

Rice and beans, cooked together with a little meat or fish or other flavourings, played a staple part in the preparation of many of their dishes in West Africa, and still do today in the West Indies. Pigeon, no-eye or black-eyed peas are amongst the many local names they use in the different islands; they also were probably native to Africa and were fortunately incredibly adaptable to surviving in different climates. Evidence of the seeds was found in an Egyptian tomb of the XIIth Dynasty; from there they spread into tropical West Africa where they became a feature of the West Africans' diet, which was then carried with them across to the New World with the slave trade.

Rice and peas are prepared throughout the islands but always with a slightly different ingredient or emphasis. In Trinidad they use pigeon peas, calling them 'congo' or 'goongoo' peas, instead of the red kidney beans preferred by Jamaican cooks. The rice may be cooked in a meat stock or coconut milk. Sometimes tinned beans are substituted and added towards the end of the cooking time but, for the purists, the beans or peas must be soaked beforehand and allowed to plump up in their own good time, which may mean overnight. It is said that the purpose of soaking is to shorten the cooking time, thus helping to reduce the complex sugars that lead to problems of flatulence. However, to really reduce the problem considerably, the water the beans have been soaking in must be thrown away, then they must be put into a fresh pot of cold water and brought to the boil. The beans must be strained again and that liquid thrown away also. Begin again by putting the beans in cold water with a pinch of bicarbonate of soda, bring to the boil and simmer until they are soft.

Linda Wolfe, a contemporary writer on Caribbean food, says that as far as the preparation of the dish 'peas an' rice' is concerned, every cook is on her own. Jamaica is the exception, for there coconut milk is an essential requirement. I have found no records that say when coconut milk was first used to cook rice, vegetables and meats in, but it was an inspired culinary leap, for it can transform a very ordinary dish into a rich experience indeed. Sweet or hot peppers, bacon or salted meats, onions or chives are additional flavourings.

Here is an account of the 'Watchman', a Jamaican recipe and very interesting for its use of the coconut 'meat', which is the grated white flesh as well as the milk which is wrung from it.

For the **Watchman** for four to six people you will need 200 g (7 oz) of ready prepared red kidney beans (keep the water they were cooked in, or the juice from the tin). Cube 250 g (8 oz) of beef or dice the same amount of lean bacon, chop 1 onion, de-seed a hot red pepper and chop 2 tomatoes. Make 2 cups of coconut milk (see Cook's Notes) and reserve the grated meat of the coconut. Take 400 g (13 oz) of raw rice and 2 tablespoons of vegetable or coconut oil. Sauté the beef in the oil to brown and add the onions. When they are soft put your beans in a very large pot and heat them up. If you are using them from a tin, keep the liquid and add water to bring the liquid content up to 1.2 litres (2 pints); otherwise keep the liquid that the beans were cooked in and top up. Add all the remaining ingredients and stir together well. Bring to the boil, then simmer very slowly with a well-fitting lid until the rice is tender. I have found that you will need to taste for seasoning, because depending on whether or not you used the beef or bacon, you will need to adapt the amount of salt you add. Jamaican cooks have told me that they never touch the pot during its cooking time, except to taste the rice to see if it is cooked. Instead they prefer to let the bottom of the pot 'bun' or burn slowly. This way you get perfectly cooked rice, and a delicious hint of 'bunned' rice at the bottom of the pot.

Upon arrival in the West Indian islands, the African learnt to adapt his agrarian skills to the plantation system. The slave owners quickly discovered that it was cheaper to allow the slaves to feed themselves than to pay for expensive imported foodstuffs for them, and throughout the islands, particularly on the large estates, they provided 'grounds' on which the slaves might grow food for their own needs.

Any surplus food or 'provisions' that the slaves produced, they were allowed to sell in the local markets. Since Sunday was their only free day, that became the established 'market day' until emancipation. It was a scene of great bustle and excitement, the activity building up through from the Saturday night. People would arrive by all manner of transport possible, carrying their garden produce on their backs or, where they had accumulated enough money to afford it, they would use donkeys or mules. Roads were few and far between and often difficult to travel on in the rainy season, so where the markets were near to the sea or rivers, great numbers of people would arrive by the local dug-out canoes, 'battoes', full of fruit and vegetables. The big estates often had markets *in situ* and some still exist on those same sites today.

The women who sold their produce on the road or in the market place were known as higglers and were allowed to keep their earnings. When the smaller estate owners were in need of extra money, they would sometimes borrow from their slaves, or following disasters such as hurricanes, they would send their slaves out on to the roads to higgle small imported consumer goods. While the weather was good, the slaves took to market yams, 'cocoes', dosheen and eddoes amongst other edible root crops; also, sweet potato, cassava, plantain, breadfruit, corn-on-the-cob and fruit. Those fortunate enough to have the opportunity or to have developed sufficient capitalist skills, might also have sold small livestock such as pigs and poultry.

By eight in the morning, the cooks from the Great House had left the market, carrying the greens in their baskets. Behind them ran porters; the boys who carried the baskets of 'white vegetables', the oxtail for the daily stockpot, the meat and fish. At the Great House all their provisions 'would be washed and arranged in bowls and dishes, upon a table on the kitchen verandah. There were always plantains, avocado pears, christophene, lettuce and watercress.' Seven different varieties of fresh beans could also be bought at the market at different seasons of the year. The 'white vegetables' were potatoes, yams, dasheen tannia eddoes, artichokes, topi tambos and sweet potatoes.

Agriculture still does play a major role in the way of life of the Africans' descendants. Herskovits, who lived and worked as an anthropologist in the West Indies, spending most of his time in Trinidad, noted in the 1930s that the divisions of labour between men and women in general followed African custom. 'Men cut the brush and prepare the ground, both men and women plant, and women do the weeding.' He also noticed indications of the old patterns adapting to the new, 'When men gather the coconuts, the women still remove the white flesh or "meat".'

In the more remote country areas the market scene has also not changed so very much from that day to this. The fruit and vegetables are laid out in piles of confusing colours and intriguing shapes and sizes. Great fibrous stems of green bananas lie about the floor. Everywhere heaps of green coconuts give a background to the smaller piles of green oranges, red peppers, yellow plantains, mysterious brown root vegetables with their root fibres still attached, and enormous pumpkins dwarfing the surrounding produce. The women sit easily on the floor or low stools, bent forward from the hips, backs quite straight, broad faces framed by the African-style headcloth. Talk, laughter, gossip and *comesse* swell and rise with the sun. The heat becomes tremendous and bears down on the scene remorselessly.

At midday, pots of food are heated right there on the spot. One such style of dish is *metagee*, a fascinating example of the Africans' delight in blending together their taste for salt and pepperiness by using salted meats and hot peppers to flavour, with their seasonal vegetables and coconut milk. You will find two or more of these combinations in nearly all of their dishes, which so typifies Afro-Caribbean food. Indeed, reference was made to the use of these flavours by John Atkins, the ship's surgeon, who described the manatee he ate on the west coast of Africa as 'seasoned high, (as are all their dishes) with okra, malaguetta and bell pepper'. Grazing in inlets on aquatic weeds, the manatee was prized for its beef-like taste and crisp and delicate fat.

Mrs Carmichael, who accompanied her husband to the West Indies at the beginning of the eighteenth century to run an estate in Trinidad, observed the Africans preparing meat with peppers and vegetables grown locally for a dish that appeared to have been brought from Africa. It seemed to be a simple version because she saw that the only vegetable used was the eddoe. She wrote, 'It abounds upon every estate. The root is not unlike a rough irregular potatoe:- the leaves make excellent wholesome greens, and the negro, with the addition of a bit of salt fish, or salt pork, has an excellent pot of soup . . .' Peppers still seemed to be the ascendant taste, for she continued, 'Capsicums – his seasoning for all dishes – they are never wanting . . . Every variety of capsicum is to be found upon a West Indian estate; indeed, they are almost a weed.' She went on to say that this soup was palatable to all Creoles – white, free, coloured or slave – and 'indeed, is one of the great blessings of the West Indies'.

Today the blend of spices and different meats remain the same, but the variety of vegetables available now throughout the year make the *metagee* all the more interesting.

Once the ingredients for **Metagee** are all assembled and prepared, there is a rhythm in the cooking of it, as you will see. For four to six people you will need to soak 180 g (6 oz) of diced salt beef and 375 g (12 oz) of saltfish overnight; pour boiling water over them. Next day drain them; the saltfish should bone and flake easily. Prepare 750 ml (1½ pints) of coconut milk (see Cook's Notes), then assemble the ingredients. These might be 1 small diced onion, 2 spring onions – known on the islands as *sives* – 2 garlic cloves, coconut oil for frying, 375 g (12 oz) of green banana, crushed black pepper, 2 tablespoons of parsley, 3 seasoning peppers, 3 leaves of 'fat pork' (which is a very broad, fleshy-leafed variety of thyme found in the West Indies) or 3 sprigs of thyme (or half of each), 6 medium okra, 2 medium potatoes (Irish or sweet, or one of each), 1 ripe plantain, 500 g (1 lb) of pumpkin and 3 large tomatoes. Fry the diced onions, garlic and beef in coconut oil. Once the onions and garlic are cooked through, add the saltfish, the peeled and chopped green banana and seasoning. Stir well. Now peel and dice all the remaining vegetables into 2 cm (¾ inch) cubes and add to the pot as you do each one in turn, beginning with the potatoes which take the longest to cook, following on with the plantain and okra, and ending with the pumpkin, which cooks in the shortest time. Pour in the coconut milk, using more if you need to, cover with a lid and cook for twenty minutes over a moderate heat. Test the vegetables, taste for salt and serve. I like the vegetables just cooked, not falling into an indistinguishable mush

John Atkins had observed the West African taste for lacing dishes with palm oil and recorded its use in a dish he had tasted called 'Black Soupee'. He wrote, 'It was a favourite dish as well at our factories as among the Negros; we make it of flesh and fowl stewed sweet, with some uncommon tasting herbs; but the ascendant taste is Pepper,

Okra and Palm oil. At first I thought it disagreeable, but custom reconciled it as the best in the country.' In the West Indies coconut oil became the regular substitute, but it is just as distinct in flavour.

The coconut palm proliferates throughout the Caribbean and is now the most widely cultivated of all the palms. There is much confusion about the uses it is put to, and even more controversy surrounds its origins. At the time of the discovery of the New World it was confined to growing in a small area of the Pacific coast of Central America, and today the evidence lies in favour of Indo-Pacific origins.

Our images of the coconut palm are usually stereotyped and consist of romantically grouped trees, their silhouetted fronds fanning out on the top of each tall unbranched trunk in feathered circles, set against all the drama of a fiery tropical sunset. This romantic memory was dispelled after I had spent an afternoon with a local woman who lived alone and did all the work herself. She was setting about the laborious task of extracting oil from the curd inside coconuts, unaware that she was involved in one of the oldest seed-crushing industries in the world.

We sat in her kitchen, a perilously hung wooden structure at the back of her tiny house, which looked for all the world like Babi Yaga's hut. Its frail bent old supporting legs appeared almost lively, as if they would suddenly skip off down the valley. Absorbing her daily life through half-closed eyes, I watched some children return with jugs of water from the stand pipe a half mile or so away to refresh a much valued, but dried up old sheep.

In her front yard exotic bushes supported household needs; double-headed hibiscus nodded down at the fresh washing spread on its branches to dry. Between the branches of the croton bush, with its long thin leaves smudged with reds, greens and yellow – the edges curling corkscrew fashion – were trays of red sorrel petals, drying in order to be steeped in boiling water and made into the traditional drink for Christmas. Below the bushes the chickens constantly scratched while the cockerels hovered close by crowing, as they do here night and day, to ensure the hens will not forget them, as if their remarkable plumage and red-hued comb could escape their attention for one moment.

Having already gathered in fifty coconuts, the woman began to grate the meat from inside the shell with a traditional hand-made grater – a sturdy wooden frame, some 30 x 60 cm, supporting a metal sheet punctured all over with small holes. Old treasured plastic buckets began to fill with the grated meat, which she then covered with water and began to wash as if it were the laundry. With many a deft, strong wring of her hands, the watery milk was squeezed out and the discarded flesh taken by some children up the road to feed the pigs.

One bucket of milk that had already been made from twenty-five coconuts and left to stand overnight appeared to have fermented, a scum of oatmeal-coloured suds rising to the top with a little of the oil already beginning to separate. This she skimmed off, then she threw out the remaining liquid, putting the oil and suds into a heavy iron pot over a raging fire fuelled with the coconut husks. While stirring it constantly, the woman explained to me that if the moon was quite full, she would have got less oil, but since the moon 'was only half way to filling itself', we would get more. The way round the problem of the full moon was to squeeze some lime juice into the mixture while it stood overnight, which helped it to 'fermen'. The pot spat out the excess water with great ferocity, as the strong winter north easterlies fanned the fire and bent the tops of the spring-green cane grass.

After an hour had passed, the scum had sunk to the bottom of the pot, having turned to a brown grainy substance (which the children love to eat), leaving the oil clear and ready to bottle once it was cool. I will always remember that this enormously time-consuming effort produced only three bottles of oil.

However, I think frying eggs in coconut oil is the finest way you can cook a fresh egg straight from the hen's nest.

For **Eggs in Coconut Oil** heat a generous amount of coconut oil in a heavy pan, crack the eggs and cook over the lowest possible heat with a heavy lid over the top. Lift out with a spatula and serve with fresh brown bread. The combination of tastes is quite delicious.

It is not clear when the African began to fry his meats in the combination of coconut oil or sugar, to give the meat its characteristic sweetish Caribbean flavour, but the following recipe for caramelized chicken uses the technique for heating coconut oil and browning the sugar until it is caramelized; then the fowl meat is fried in it, before stewing it in the spices with tomatoes and okras.

Caramelized Chicken is a simple and very traditional preparation of a fowl. For four people season four chicken legs in 1–2 tablespoons of prepared seasoning (see Cook's Notes), rub well in under the skin and leave for a minimum of six hours. Take a little coconut oil, 1 tablespoon of brown sugar, 1 very finely chopped onion, 1 crushed clove of garlic, 1 chopped seasoning pepper, 3–4 tablespoons of tomato sauce, 2 large chopped tomatoes, 6–8 okras, salt and black pepper to taste. Once marinaded, wipe the pieces of chicken dry, spread the oil across the bottom of the pan and sprinkle the brown sugar over it. Heat until it caramelizes to a good rich brown, stirring as it does so as to mix it together. Then carefully drop in the chicken pieces and turn, watching carefully that the caramel does not burn. When they are golden brown all over, lower the heat, add the onions, garlic, seasoning pepper and a little salt. Let it all sweat with a lid on. Fifteen minutes before the chicken is cooked add the tomato sauce and well-chopped tomatoes and okras. Serve with boiled plantain and rice.

Vegetable foods had played a very important role in the feeding of the population in West Africa from the Middle Ages. Gustavus wrote, 'The land produces all kinds of vegetables in great abundance.' The three main staples were yam, plantain and Indian corn; on these the African slave depended for his very survival in the New World, and they all had been part of the everyday diet in Africa. From the dishes made with them, one can see how very strongly Caribbean cuisine is rooted in African food.

Of the three, the most important food was invariably the yam, which was indigenous to West Africa. In the Middle Ages al-Omari wrote, 'They cultivate a plant called al-quafi; these are soft roots which they bury in the ground and leave until they grow hard.' New varieties were later introduced by the Portuguese in the fifteenth and sixteenth centuries and later travellers commented on the fact that boiled or pounded yam was the diet of both king and slave.

Great yam festivals were held to celebrate its planting and later the harvest; Gustavus remembered, 'We compute the day in which the sun crosses the line, and on its setting that evening there is a great shout throughout the land.'

A neighbour, upon handing me some of her freshly harvested yams, once explained to me the traditions that still surround the planting. Again the phases of the moon are all-important; some yams demand a waxing moon, others a waning one. Otutu yams should be planted three days after the full moon, Guinea yams after the first quarter, red yams 'from the new moon down, in between moon changes', while if Ibo yams are planted at 'full moon today, tomorrow put them down the hole and they'll come up fine and nice'.

Today the West Indian still prizes his yam and some varieties even carry the old African names, such as the white otutu or yellow Guinea yam. It requires much hard work, mostly done by hand, to raise the earth into mounds or ridges into which the 'setts', taken from the top of the tubers, are carefully planted towards the end of the dry season. Very often they intercrop with maize and okra.

In Africa, just as they made *fou-fou* from boiled and pounded plantain or cassava, so they sometimes did with the yam when it was harvested. They would peel the yam, then cut it into small pieces; after boiling it until tender, it was then pounded in a wooden mortar to make a glutinous dough which, if they could afford it, was dipped into a sauce or stew. It might have been thought that these basic dishes were produced either because it was a cheap way to feed the slave population, or because today it fills a gap where people are poor. However, the African and the Afro-Caribbean still relish their traditional ways with *fou-fou* or *cou-cou*, which is made from corn meal. When Ellen Wilson wrote a West African cookbook in 1971, she told the story of a visiting scholar who was asked what people ate in his country. The cry was, after listing a range of meat, bread and fish: 'What no porridge, this is starvation.'

Perhaps because of their appearance, yams do not attract the attention they deserve in the north. I believe that it is also because they are quite different when pulled straight from the ground and cooked. When buying yams, see that there are no blemishes and ask if they are fresh. The following recipes, both given to me in the West Indies, make the best of them.

For **Baked Yams** for four people you will need 2 yams weighing 500 g (1 lb) each, flour for dredging, salt, 45 g (1½ oz) of butter, 3 tablespoons of milk and black pepper. Peel the yams, cut them in half, then lengthways. Mix the flour with the salt and pepper; roll the yams in this and bake in a fairly hot oven. Test after forty to forty-five minutes, as you would for a baked potato, to see if it is cooked. The skin will have formed into a hard shell. When cool enough cut one side about 5 cm (2 inches) wide along the length of the yam, scoop out the flesh and mash with good butter and the milk. If necessary add more milk, salt and pepper. Put back in the shells and place under the grill to brown.

For **Grilled Yams** buy in quantities as you would ordinary potatoes. Peel the yams and put them in cold salted water. Bring to the boil, lower the heat and test after twenty minutes or so with a sharp knife to see if they are tender. Drain, slice and put them under the grill or over a charcoal fire. Brown on both sides and serve with melted butter.

The plantain, a relative of the banana family, originated in southern India, and was also introduced to the West Indies via West Africa soon after the discovery of the New World. To the uninitiated eye, the fruit on the stem looks much the same, if perhaps slightly larger, than a banana. They have been described as giant tree-like perennial herbs and grow in what are locally called 'stools', clumps of shoots of suckers that turn upwards from the stump. Within nine to eighteen months the tree reaches maturity and the broad sheaves of green leaves curve down over the stem, from which grow the whorls of green bananas. Each stem bears anything from fourteen to twenty-seven kilograms of fruit in its short life, and many of the islands depend on the income that comes from growing and exporting them to countries in the north. They are also appreciated locally for being highly nutritious. Do not be put off by the sometimes blackened appearance of the skin. In the West Indies they are cooked at varying degrees of ripeness, from green to half-ripe and ripe. The following recipe is for a fairly ripe plantain. Don't hesitate to seek advice when you buy.

 To cook **Plantain** allow half a plantain for each person as they are quite rich. Cut them in half, leaving the skin on, and put them into cold water and bring to the boil. They usually take about fifteen minutes, but test after ten minutes with a knife for softness. Peel and serve, or you can cut the two halves in two again, press flat very gently and sauté them in butter.

Much importance is still attached to the planting of corn too. It is talked about with deep concern as the time approaches, and there is anxiety over whether the rains will come on time or not. The local calendar for planting begins in March to April, when the land is cleaned or cutlashed. Then, in May to June, the corn is planted. It is carefully watched over and the growth of the straight green stems calls for daily reports on its progress. In July they say, 'They're growin now. You haven't much to do.' In August and September the weeding has to be done; in October, more weeding; then the harvest of the ripe corn. As its moment of ripening approaches, presents of the young ears are made. On many evenings we share fresh young corn with our neighbour under the canopy of stars, watching the intensity of light from the glowing charcoals freshen and die as the night sea breezes occasionally stir them. Much of the corn crop is dried in December; if there are no rats about, it is sometimes left to dry on the stalk. Otherwise it is picked, the leaves folded back, then tied together in bundles and hung out of the reach of the rats in the sun, later to be ground and fed to the chickens. One soon becomes accustomed to the gentle starting-up of the corn-grinding machine. The people in our village shred the corn with a knife into an old enamel bowl; it is part of the heartbeat of the village.

In the West Indies, when the landowner planted corn, he would hire groups of men at the beginning of the season to do the reaping. In Trinidad they called such a group a *gayap*. As they worked, a kalenda drum – the traditional accompaniment to stick fighting – was beaten, and the men sang songs which eased their task; the rhythms, which were born in Africa, doubtless lightened their hearts, while the words evoked memories of old.

> Rain can't wet me
> When I have my fighting stick in my hand
> Rain can't wet me
> I advancing on the foe like a roaring lion

These *gayap* songs were also used to make oblique comments on the foibles of various villagers, or to ridicule the landowner or the world at large. Herskovits claimed the *gayap* to be a lineal descendant of an institution in the kingdom of Dahomey called *dokpwe*. It was an example of a custom carried over because it was immediately applicable to the requirements of the slave system, where gang labour was fundamental to the working of the estates.

Corn was also an important crop for the Africans in their homeland. Arab history claims to have had the seed by the twelfth century and carried it into Africa which, until then, had always depended on the cultivation of sorghum. However, it was probably the Portuguese who took the seed into West Africa in the fifteenth century. At the height of the slave trade in the seventeenth and eighteenth centuries it was a major cash crop that was used to provision the slave ships and factories where they were kept. I have read some extremely interesting papers recently, on excavations carried out in Barbados into some of the graves of the slave population on the Newton plantation. Until now, research has relied on written and oral sources, but from the skeletal remains of jaws and teeth interred in the seventeenth and eighteenth centuries, one can tell that slaves often went through alternating periods of severe vitamin deficiency and seemed to survive on a diet solely of corn.

In the Africa the slaves left behind, there had been many dishes based on corn, and a variation of these came to the Caribbean. There was sweet and salt *pemi*, considered a delicacy, and *cachop*, which was a special food of the Yarriba. Both were based on corn meal but the latter was baked in an earthenware pot that was placed on a tripod made of three stones over a fire. *Sansam* was a dish of pounded corn mixed with salt and sugar and eaten quite dry.

Cou-cou was a simple preparation of corn meal with the occasional added luxury of okra, or ladies fingers, to cheer things up and make the rather dry quality of the dish more palatable. It could be cooked quickly in one pan over the coal pot.

 If you wish to make **Cou-Cou**, the quantities for four to six people are 500 g (1 lb) of fine yellow corn meal, 600 ml (1 pint) of water, 1 teaspoon of salt, 2 tablespoons of vegetable oil and 60 g (2 oz) of butter. Use 30 g (1 oz) of the butter in cooking and the other at the end to coat the surface. Bring the water to the boil and sprinkle the meal over it with the salt. Allow the water to boil for a few minutes longer, stirring carefully all the time to prevent lumps occurring. Once all the lumps have gone, the butter can be added, which makes it easier to swallow. Opinion as to how long the corn meal should be stirred varies considerably, from ten to fifty minutes.

Cou-cou may well be a later and thicker version of loblolly. Apparently in the very early days on the estates the African would cry out, 'Oh! Oh! no more loblolly'.

Bajans like to think their present-day dish, *conkie*, has its roots in *kenkey* – an African sourdough bread of steamed cornmeal dough – and so it probably does, but life has become more prosperous and now they add grated coconut, sweet potato or pumpkin, raisins and spices to the fresh ground corn meal, which they no longer 'sour' first, but still steam in the same way.

The African, unable to get his *kenkey* and revulsed by the loblolly, often preferred to roast the fresh ears of corn over hot coals and still carries on this custom today, seated at the side of the road in the evening, with his fresh corn roasting on the coal pot, ready to sell.

At Christmas time, the most important crop is black-eyed or pigeon peas. The task of shelling them is shared by young and old alike, who appear from nowhere and all sit down until the job is done, passing the time by gossiping, discussing whether the peas had had enough rain or not, and relishing the many ways in which they might prepare them.

One way is in coconut milk, or with rice, or in water, with a little piece of salted meat to flavour. Among these, stewed peas in coconut milk are a particular passion.

To make **Pigeon Peas in Coconut Milk** for four people you ideally need 500 g (1 lb) of fresh peas, but dried ones soaked overnight are also good. You also need vegetable oil for frying, 1 medium onion, 2 cloves of garlic, 2 spring onions, black pepper, 250 g (½ lb) of mixed salted meats such as salt beef, smoked bacon, pig's tail or salted pork ribs and 600 ml (1 pint) of fresh coconut milk (or just enough to cover). Chop the onion, garlic and meats into very small pieces and cook them in the oil until the onions are soft; add the shelled peas, stir around, then cover with the coconut milk. Simmer with the lid on until the peas are soft. You might try adding a little sugar at the end of the cooking time. This dish could be served alone for the mixtures complement each other very well.

I am equally as fond of **Peas with Salted Pork,** which is also good made with lentils. For four people soak 250 g (8 oz) of dried pigeon peas or green lentils overnight. Have prepared 250 g (8 oz) of diced salted pork, 2 tablespoons each of very finely chopped onions, carrots, celery and parsley, 2 cloves of garlic, olive oil for frying, 1½ tablespoons of tomato ketchup, salt and pepper and the juice of a fresh lime. Use a heavy pot with a well-fitting lid. Fry the chopped onions, crushed garlic and vegetables in a little olive oil, add the drained lentils and pork, then cover with boiling water and the tomato ketchup. Add salt and pepper to taste, but be careful since the salt in the pork may be enough. Simmer for approximately one and a half hours or until the lentils are soft. To serve, squeeze in a few drops of fresh lime juice.

The African left behind him villages that have been described as 'occasional beads on a thread of a tribal trail. There is a rhythm in the sequence . . . a cluster of villages, a series of gardens – a true stretch of forest – a clearing . . . where the village clearing lies in a river of light between the forest way-beside the garden clearings.' Here he grew peanuts, sometimes known as earthnuts or ground nuts, which were a fundamental crop in West Africa. Ibn Battuta, during his journeying in Mali, observed that 'the natives extract from the ground a grain which looks like a bean; they roast it and eat it, the taste being like that of roasted chick peas. Sometimes they grind this grain to make a kind of round spongy dough which they fry.' He also wrote that he had seen it ground to a flour and sweet cakes made from it. The peanut had been widely distributed throughout the West Indian islands in pre-Columbian times, and it was the Portuguese who had taken them back across the Atlantic and introduced them into the Africans' diet. When the Africans arrived in the West Indies, their experience of growing the crop was such that they simply continued to plant, harvest and cook with it in their traditional way.

It is an important crop in the West Indies today for exporting. In St Vincent, where I have seen it growing, it fascinates me because of the extraordinary way it sets out to help itself: the soil must be kept loose around it since, when the seed is set, the flower stem elongates and turns downwards, forcing the young fruit beneath the soil, from where it takes all its nourishment. It is most curious to pick. The thin brown roots pull up very easily and delicately; attached along them are numerous pale cream nuts, looking rather like very new small potatoes, pulled weeks too soon. Both in West Africa and the West Indies it is mostly the work of the women to harvest them. Once done, the nutshells are generally scrubbed and laid on a tray to dry in the sun, or sometimes they are shelled and then ground, or simply placed in a flat tin over an open fire and roasted.

Groundnut chop is a classic stew in West Africa, and the following version reflects all the old influences that travelled back and forth across the Atlantic and survived through many generations to this day. Chicken or smoked fish are sometimes substituted for the beef.

To make **Groundnut Chop**, you will need for the sauce 90 g (3 oz) of raw peanuts, half a teaspoon of grated fresh ginger, 2 teaspoons of brown sugar, a few drops of hot pepper sauce, 3 teaspoons of fresh lime juice, 1 tablespoon of coconut oil and 125–150 ml (4 fl oz) of water. First prepare 250 g (8 oz) of beef by cutting it against the grain into strips 5 mm (⅛ inch) thick. You will then need 90 g (3 oz) pig's trotter, 50 ml (¾ pint) of cold water, 1 large onion, 2 medium tomatoes, 2 seasoning peppers, black pepper and salt to taste, 4 cloves of crushed garlic, a handful of freshly chopped parsley and 2–3 sprigs of fresh thyme. Chop all the ingredients, put them into a pot and cover with the water; bring to the boil (it may be necessary to skim the top of the water once or twice), then simmer. Blend together all the ingredients for the sauce and add to the stew. Simmer with a lid on so that the sauce gradually thickens until the meat is tender. Remove the pig's trotter to serve if you wish.

It is not entirely clear when a greater variety of recipes and foodstuffs filtered down to the slave population, but gradually the pattern of life and food in the slave quarters and the Great House became inextricably woven together, as did the relationships between master and slave. It was well after emancipation and probably into this century before the slaves could afford many of the imported provisions. Mrs Carmichael wrote that on her estate the slaves grew produce in such abundance that with their surplus they were able to barter for everything produced locally which they may have fancied, ranging from bread and salted meats to fresh poultry, game and fish.

The most interesting of the many travellers' accounts of visits to the estates is a diary – 10,000 pages in length – kept by one Thomas Thistlewood, who lived in Jamaica from 1750 to 1786. Slowly he rose from fairly humble work to become an overseer and finally a landowner with his own estate and slaves. Recently discovered in Lincolnshire, it gives a unique insight into life in Jamaica at that time.

On arrival at Savannah La Mar, Thistlewood was given a job supervising a pen, providing foodstuffs for slaves and feed for the animals. It carried a variety of livestock, large and small, from cattle to sheep, goats, pigs, ducks, turkeys and fowls. In this job he mixed almost entirely with the slaves and learnt a good deal from them about the local flora and fauna. A new 'private pasture' was bought during his time there, which enabled him to indulge his horticultural curiosity and to compare local methods with those familiar to him in England. He cultivated a bed of Battersea asparagus seeds, cabbage, savoys, broccoli, turnips, peas and pumpkins, with considerable success. He wrote that he had succeeded with at least thirty-five sorts of trees, including sweet-and-sour oranges locally known as *sybilles*, a grape arbour and twenty varieties or more of herbs and spices.

From another account by Mrs Carmichael, we can see that the African benefited from the success of experiments by people such as Thistlewood, and was now able to grow more than just his 'ground provisions'. She wrote, 'Sweet pot herbs are at all times to be found in the Negro's ground: sweet marjoram grows luxuriantly; thyme is more difficult to rear, but mint and sage and marjoram grow readily, by merely sticking a sprig in the ground.'

Post from England was not the only way that planters such as Thistlewood came by their seeds. The mango, cultivated in India for more than four thousand years, had arrived in Barbados a few years before Thistlewood, from Brazil; the Portuguese had introduced it into West Africa before taking it across to the New World. In Jamaica in 1782, Thistlewood benefited from the capture of a French ship by the British, and was given two mango seeds wrapped in wax, looking 'remarkably fresh'. The finest now cultivated in the West Indies is the 'Julie', which was once described as a ball of tow soaked in turpentine and molasses. Now, after years of dedicated cultivation, the stringy texture has been bred out and the flesh is delicious and smooth.

In the evenings Thistlewood would sit down to eat with his slaves. In one of his earliest entries he describes how he dined with 'old Sharper who is a sensible Negro'. They had clucking hen and pepperpot (see pp. 54 and 35) and *duckanoo*; also *tum tum*, which was plantain and fish beaten together. If they were not fortunate enough to have some fish, then they just boiled and pounded the plantain into *fou-fou*. This is the first reference I have ever found of the English eating a very African dish as part of their meal, and was the beginning of the marriage that we find in the West Indies today of foods from different cultures being served together at the same table.

I am giving the recipe for *dukanoo* here because, although it is unlikely you will make it, it is interesting. The first reference I found to it being prepared in the West Indies was in the middle of the seventeenth century. Since the slaves rarely had plates, banana leaves were used to wrap the mixture in. Greaseproof paper can be used instead, but the leaves do add a particular flavour.

 To make **Dukanoo** – or **Duckna** as it can be known – you will need patience, for the banana leaves in which to wrap the mixture have to be found first. These must be steamed for a few minutes to make the leaf soft and pliable, otherwise it will split when you tie the mixture up in it as you would a parcel. Cut the leaves into squares of approximately 23 cm (9 inches) square. To make the filling for ten to twelve parcels you will need 175 g (6 oz) of grated sweet potato, 1 small grated coconut, salt and sugar to taste, a little grated nutmeg, half a teaspoon of vanilla, 4 tablespoons of vegetable oil, 60 g (2 oz) of flour and enough milk to mix. Mix all these ingredients together until, as they say here, 'the mixture drop off' (in other words, you have a thick batter). Drop approximately 2 tablespoons in the centre of each leaf and fold carefully, then tie with strings made from the centre stem of the banana leaf which is fibrous and tears into strings very easily. Steam them for around thirty to forty minutes. If there were no sweet potatoes, they substituted the ubiquitous ground corn meal.

Thistlewood soon took a field slave, Marina, as his 'wife'. It was customary for the white estate owners and overseers to have sexual relations with all their slaves, but she became a special favourite. In Thistlewood's case, he showed it by taking special care of her with presents of rum, beef and pepperpot. Sometimes he would treat all the negroes to extra corn allowances so that they could make *fungi* or *cou-cou* as the Bajans called it. After one such gift, he wrote in his diary, 'They were very merry all night.'

As time passed, Thistlewood's relationship with Marina deepened so much that he built her a small cottage and for a house present gave her an iron cassava roaster, an updated iron version of the Amerindians' flat disk with a small lip all the way round. He also stocked up her kitchen with gifts of wild cinnamon, a barrel of beef brine with a piece of beef in it and some potatoes.

Thistlewood kept a record of his distribution of coal pots to each household, and through this one can see how the slaves were accommodated and relationships formed. Its use would not have come as a complete surprise to the slaves. We know from Gustavus, as he journeyed to the African coast through the lands of Tinmah after his kidnapping, that he was 'very much struck with this difference . . . they cooked their provisions in an iron pot'.

These pots were also used when the slaves got together for their own entertainment. As time went by, there was much more freedom of movement for the slaves than has generally been supposed. They were given 'tickets' to travel about by road and river on estate business and their own, and they assembled regularly to eat, dance and talk. Although they were forbidden to speak their own varied languages, they must have had as much to share and exchange about themselves as the planters did; their work in the fields, their past and their hopes and fears about what was going to happen to them. Preparing foods together must have provoked shared confidences too, and the rum supplied on occasions must have increased the company's nostalgia.

A 'cook-up' is a traditional example of the kind of dish made for such holiday and festive occasions, or today, for when a group of people suddenly feel inspired to hold a get-together, perhaps to go to the beach on a Sunday, taking the prepared pot with them. It does mean finding a very large iron pot to hold all the ingredients. Today, people try to include more meat than they would have done in the past, especially if it is a special occasion. If a chicken, cow or pig, or all three, have been freshly killed in the village that day, parts of them may be thrown in. The following recipe, by Sylvia Hunt, re-creates the flavours of this traditional festive 'one pot' which has survived through the generations. It is said to have links with a similar dish, still prepared to this day in West Africa, called jollof rice, possibly because it originated with a tribe from the Gambia called the Wolof.

 For a **Cook-Up** for four to six people you will need 500 g (1 lb) each of diced fresh pork and beef, and 1.5 kg (3 lbs) of chopped chicken pieces, sugar and oil for frying, 2 medium onions, salt and black pepper to taste, 500 g (1 lb) of cooked pigeon peas, 250 ml (8 fl oz) of tomato sauce, 1 seasoning pepper, 250 ml (8 fl oz) of coconut milk, 500 g (1 lb) of rice and enough chicken stock for it to cook in. For the meat marinade you will need to blend together three bunches of spring onions, 2 kg (4 lbs) onions, 1 stick of celery, 2–3 sprigs of thyme, 1 tablespoon of chopped coriander, 4 cloves of garlic, 1 bay leaf, 3 cm (1 inch) length of grated ginger, 2 teaspoons of brown sugar, salt to taste, 125–150 ml (4 fl oz) of rum and the same again of wine or cider vinegar. I was told to mince all these marinade ingredients, except the rum, but it is easier to blend them mechanically. This mixture can be made well beforehand and what you do not use will keep if well sealed in the refrigerator. Rub the cut up meats well with fresh lime and water. Dry off, and rub in the marinade and chill for at least two to four hours (overnight is better), particularly if you are unsure of the tenderness of the meat, which is sometimes the case in the tropics. Dry the meat very carefully, removing all traces of the seasoning, and fry in sugar and oil until golden brown. Add the salt and black pepper. Let the meats sweat out all their juices on a moderately high heat for about ten minutes, add the onions, then lower the heat to a simmer. As you may imagine this is quite an art over a wood fire, but all the locals are unconsciously expert at cooking in this way. Cover with a lid and when the chicken is done remove it from the pot and set aside. When the beef and pork are thoroughly cooked add the cooked pigeon peas, tomato sauce, chopped seasoning pepper and the coconut milk. Let the mixture reduce by a third, then add the washed rice with enough chicken stock for it to cook in. Keep a well-fitting lid firmly on while the rice is cooking, stirring occasionally to stop it sticking. As the rice grains swell, add more stock, a little at a time. Just before the rice is cooked, put back the chicken pieces and test for saltiness.

I have not found any records written by the planters describing their slaves' festivities, other than an account by Thistlewood. On one occasion he gave a day off and extra rations of a barrel of mackerel, a pint of rum and some sugar to each slave. He wrote next day, 'they drummed and danced all night long.' This always provoked him into a state of anxiety and he invariably seems to have flogged them the following day.

Many of the strongest African feast traditions have a religious origin. The first yield of any plant was always taken to the church to be blessed by the minister, then thrown away as an offering to the members of the family who had died. Some go as far as to say it is for the *jumbie* or ancestral spirits. These played an important part in the preparations on the night of any wedding. Drums would beat in the village, while offerings were prepared. Folks would remember: 'They kill fowl, some does kill goat, and kill pig, big so too.' White rice, yams and other vegetables were also cooked. Some of the rice and blood from the kill would be prepared separately without salt, and be mixed with parched and ground corn and sugar as a special offering for the spirits. At the stroke of midnight an old man would collect these offerings and go outside, crying out in Yarriba. 'Everybody don' understand what he is saying,' according to the people who spoke with Herskovits, but some were able to interpret, saying that he was recalling their ancestral past. 'All me people from Guinea, all you come. Come this we own food.' Then the offerings were dashed to the ground. He would continue, 'All we pickney from Guinea, all we from Congo come join. Join in we marry, so we all marry decide.'

Up until the 1930s, and even today in the very remote islands, the African was often able to say where he came from in Africa. The villagers of Toco, in Trinidad, told Herskovits, 'All we from Guinea, all we from the Congo, Dahomey, Benin and Ebo.' In Carriacou, the most southerly island of the Grenadines – named by the Amerindian, Kayryouacou – you will still find families who know exactly who they are and which tribe they come from. Here Bele Kawe ritual singing is, amazingly, still very African, based on the call or statement sung, followed in turn by the response. It is mostly in French patois, reflecting the earlier occupation by the French, and is based on themes of resistance and rebellion. A Bele Kawe song translated runs:

I am Claris, I have no children,
Papa God did not give me any.
Do not cry out my name in the crowd.
If they were lending
I would have borrowed one,
If they were selling
I would have bought one.

Several traditions have survived in this small island that involve feasting when there is an occasion such as mourning, celebrating a marriage, a house-moving – called a *maroon* – or even boat-building. Each family, or 'nation', performs the dance that is special to the tribe they come from, culminating in the 'big drum dance', which goes on all night. These drums, the bula, babble and fule, their goat skins stretched tight across old estate-rum kegs, give a foundation beat that underlies the forces that have survived through generations. When the dancers rise to the call of the drum, they carry the torch for their ancestors.

An African saying goes, 'The dead are never gone – they are thickening in the shadows,' and mourning is marked with a wake and 'tombstone feast'. Until recently a death was announced by young boys who travelled round the island singing: '*Ca qui tend parlez l'autre. Madame ou Monsieur mourie.*' A wake can last days and the echo of hymn-singing rebounds on every hillside. After forty days they finish with a 'tea mass', which can be a very strong refreshment indeed, such as white rum, called locally 'jackiron'.

On 'All Saints' the family light candles at night in the grove, and sit until the flame is extinguished. I have seen a whole hillside flicker with the flames of countless candles on such occasions.

When the islanders hold a *maroon*, many people gather to physically dismantle the wooden house and assemble it on a new site. On completion, the table is specially prepared with a clean cloth. A glass of rum or wine, a piece of boiled chicken and a side of pork or mutton are all carefully placed on the table, along with some matches and perhaps a cigar or cigarette. These are left for the ancestors to enjoy and are never touched until the next morning.

Elsewhere, traditions are less clear cut. But while the structure of West Indian society is firmly European, the African contribution has, as Herskovits wrote, functioned beneath the surface as a reinterpretation of African custom. Gustavus remembered: 'The head of the family usually eats alone; his wife and family also have their separate tables.' I have experienced just this in more remote villages. When we arrive, the husband goes to the kitchen and asks his wife to prepare food for us. She will bring it in but never stays, despite my protestations; and we never leave the house without her emerging to give us gifts of whatever fruit is in season.

In Carriacou, celebrations are often marked with smoked foods, and the young men with trained dogs hunt for wild goats in the hills. Other delicacies are gamy creatures such as the manicou and tatoo, which are rodents and armadillos; both are beautifully seasoned before stewing. Curried goat was introduced by the East Indian, and its popularity spread through all the islands; it is prepared for most festive occasions by almost all the different groups of people. Do not be put off by the large amounts of bone found in it, as it sweetens the dish.

 My version of **Curried Goat,** Grenadian style, is very simple but no less delicious. For four people you will need 500 g (1 lb) of goat meat, 1 heaped tablespoon of grated fresh ginger, a squeeze of lime juice and half a teaspoon of salt, 25 ml (1 fl oz) of coconut or vegetable oil, 2–3 tablespoons of white sugar, 4 garlic cloves coarsely chopped, 1 medium onion finely chopped, salt to taste, 2–3 sprigs of thyme, 2 tablespoons of curry powder and 125–150 ml (4 fl oz) of tomato sauce. If you are preparing this in the West Indies, wash the meat carefully looking out for splinters of bone. Dry the meat thoroughly, grate the ginger all over it, add the lime juice and salt. Mix in and leave for three to four hours. On a high heat let the oil and sugar caramelize, then add the meat. Remove from the heat, but do not stir for a few moments so that the meat can really become a good rich golden-brown colour. Return to the heat, stir well and let the uncrusted surfaces catch up. Cook for a further ten minutes over a moderate heat, then add the onions, garlic and salt to taste. Cover the pot and let the juices sweat for fifteen minutes. Add the thyme, curry powder and tomato sauce. Lower the heat to a gentle simmer and cook until the meat is soft. I do not add water, but I do watch the pot carefully during the cooking to see nothing sticks. The juices become thick and rich, maybe too rich for some, in which case add a little warm water every so often after the first thirty minutes to keep the sauce at the thickness of single cream.

Another example of the continuation of the African's religious experience was the forming of the groups called Shouters who, initiated to receive the Gods, would be possessed by them so that they could dance and sing and receive the spirit. On such occasions or festive gatherings the Africans danced the quadrille, reel, jig and *passé*, but did not, despite this, lose their own emphasis on rhythm and antiphony between the leader and chorus. From this, and the traditional use of song to comment on current day events – both social and political – grew the calypso, one of the best known musical forms outside the Caribbean since before the First World War. As these aboriginal African cultures were more or less stripped away in the New World, a new order developed throughout the length and breadth of the West Indian islands.

Ships' crews of the eighteenth and nineteenth centuries left us with fascinating accounts of travelling inland up the rivers that the African used to fish before his upheaval. John Atkins, a ship's surgeon, wrote after sailing up the West African coast in the middle of the eighteenth century: 'They trade by a magnificent way of living . . . the sea gives them plenty of flying fish, Barricuda, and King fish, particularly the first . . .' Apparently the sea abounded in the former which flew in great numbers into the boats, and which they took up in dip-nets and sometimes the dolphins with them. In these same waters they also caught alligators, which were bought by the ships' crews and transported alive to the West Indies, to be salted down and sold. Here, too, they caught sharks. 'We have catched three in less than half an hour, each eight to ten feet long the livers of them making above ten gallons of oil . . . Our seamen dressed them and ate the flesh tho' it is very strong.'

In the African rivers there were many bays to be found that provided a variety of good fish: 'Turtle, Mullet, Skate, Old Wives, Cavalloes, Barricudoes' and many others. The African would have found all these upon his arrival in the Caribbean and been all too familiar with their preparation. It is the descendant of those same Africans who, out of all the peoples brought here, has inherited the skills and knowledge necessary to be a fisherman. It is he who now sails in these waters and has taken possession as he sails up the coast past a chain of forts, now grey reminders of a past fraught with the European struggle to hold on to the soils that were so rich in edible white gold. And it is his face that is washed by the wind and the sea, and his eyes that watch the sea heaving up and down.

Thistlewood occasionally allowed men to go in his 'battoe' down to the seaside to go a-crabbing and fishing. This helped to reduce the expense of feeding slaves, while the master could offer his dinner guests an excellent choice of some of the best freshwater fish and seafood in the world. 'Plenty of crabs also run o'night', Thistlewood commented. On well-lit nights, men and boys still go searching for the crabs burrowed in the loose sands in the coconut groves. As the moon approaches its fullness and the first rains begin to fall, the 'mouche flay' or fireflies vie in a brilliant earthly abundance with the stars studded into a black quilted canopy above. Often a star shoots loose from its firmament, falling to earth, and is lost in the myriad amorous flashings of the mouche flays' nightly search for love. The land crab hides there, dreaming of the dawn, when he will be safe. He waits, cool in his sand burrow, until skilled hands reach straight past the lethal claw, grasp the top of his back legs at the base of the shell and pull him out. The men and boys can be seen with their gunny sacks bulging with their night's work, and will sell to you if you are lucky.

There are many species of crabs to be found in the Caribbean islands. Their colours differ widely from a pale bluish-lavender to a deeper purple, olive to a brownish-black or the pink to orange of some juveniles. They can live in the mangrove, or the coconut and banana groves, or in the cooling mud flats of the river estuaries and streams. Some carry names such as the fiddler, mangrove, calling crab or land crab, and you can find the blue or black tropical crabs sold live in the English street markets of Brixton and Dalston, or the big centre at Billingsgate. If you buy them, but do not want to eat them straight away, freeze them live and they will last well for a week or so. After that, the flesh tends to dry out. If you intend to eat them within a day or so, keep them in a bucket with a heavy lid and feed them on a little coconut meat to sweeten their flesh. Whenever you decide to eat them, be sure to clean them very carefully. They can be cooked very simply and are still delicious if you bring enough water to the boil to cover however many you are cooking, then drop them straight in and cook for three to four minutes. This is quite enough, as the flesh only needs heating through; any longer, and all the succulent taste of the sea is lost.

Here is a recipe for **Sautéd Crab** for which you may substitute the spider or ordinary sea crab from the North Atlantic. For two people pour about 4 tablespoons of good olive oil into a large heavy pan with a well-fitting lid. Cut a hot pepper in half, removing the seeds, and drop into the oil that is heating slowly. Leave it to give its chilli heat to the oil for four to five minutes and remove. Keeping the heat low, let 30 g (1 oz) of unsalted butter melt into the oil. Add half a medium onion, chopped so fine it is almost minced, with a tablespoon of equally well-chopped parsley, 2 crushed cloves of garlic, and a quarter of a teaspoon of finely grated fresh ginger (you can leave the skin on if it is very fresh). Steam through for another four to five minutes until they are quite transparent and melting into the sauce. Separate the legs and throw in the crab pieces, the shell with edible contents intact, with 140 ml (¼ pint) of good dry white wine. Add salt to your taste, raise the heat for a minute or so, stir and then lower the heat again. It is best to finish the simmering with the lid tightly on and the pan over a flame spreader. Remove after five minutes, and adjust your seasoning. This dish is best prepared a few hours before and left for the flavours to blend. Serve by warming through very gently for a few minutes.

When I watch the fishermen opening up their nets, I often think of a description by a nineteenth-century lady traveller to the West African coast, which shows us a picture of the fishing life our African left behind. She wrote:

> I am visiting Sorrow of Evening. The walls of her little bark hut are hung with a grey film of net; for she lives by the sea and her husband is a fisherman. With a seine of checkered cloth, she has been fishing in a backwater . . . and now she heaps her catch upon a mat of green leaf spread upon the clay floor . . . none are larger than an almond. Some like moonstones and some like opals; others freckled with gilt, vermillion, small bold ones striped like tigers, burn there on the banana leaf.

The fisherman will probably gladly give you the smaller reef fish that the slaves would have eaten – squirrel or butter fish, for example – because nobody wants to fiddle with the very small bones. This is precisely what makes the fish so sweet. Try the following method of cooking with fresh herring, brown, pink or salmon trout.

To **Barbecue Fish** light a fire using good charcoal. Nothing else will do. Have a small jug ready with a little olive oil and some rock salt. They are essential since they stimulate the smoke and put flavour into the fish. Unless the fish are sardines clean out the stomachs and wipe the outside with a clean damp cloth. This will help not to lose the essential flavour of the fish. Place it between two wire racks with a handle insulated so that there is no risk of burning yourself and ruining the idea of a barbecue for ever. Put the fish over the coals, which by now should be glowing. Have ready beside the fire a large bowl that will take however many fish you have cooked, and fill it with enough water to cover them. The timing will depend on how well you like your fish cooked. Since I prefer mine very lightly cooked, I would give each side of a trout five minutes, for example. Fifteen will certainly be more than enough. The skin by now will be dry and crisp. Drop the fish straight into the sea water for a minute or two, drain and serve. This is a wonderful way to keep the flesh moist.

Fish in the Caribbean waters are just as exotic in appearance and taste, especially the sailfish, thor or ocean gar, with its luminous turquoise-green skeleton. Any of these are delicious if prepared with green tomatoes.

 For **Fish with Green Tomatoes** for two people you will need 500 g (1 lb) of fish, a little coconut or good extra virgin olive oil, 3–4 green tomatoes, 2 green seasoning peppers, 1 medium onion, 4 spring onions, 1 tablespoon of fresh marjoram, black pepper and salt, a little plain flour and curry powder, and 1 large teaspoon of tomato ketchup. Remove the skin of the fish and cut into steaks 1.5 cm (½ inch) thick. The large central bone divides the segments naturally into four parts, so just ease them away from the bone with a sharp knife. On a large plate, mix enough flour to dust the fish steaks with salt and black pepper to taste and a dust of curry powder. Coat the bottom of the frying pan liberally with coconut oil, turn the steaks over on both sides in the flour mixture, place the onion cut in thin rings and the other carefully sliced ingredients in layers, and lay on the bottom of the pan. Put the fish on top and dot each steak with a quarter of a teaspoon of tomato ketchup. Cook on a moderately high heat for three minutes with a well-fitting lid, then turn the steaks (not touching the ingredients on the bottom of the pan) and cook for another minute or two.

For those who chose the sea as a living after emancipation, it defined the horizons of their life. This happened increasingly in the southern islands as commercial agriculture slumped towards the end of the nineteenth century; the women carried on sharecropping while the men took to fishing to supplement their diet. Today, father teaches son all that he knows. Where there is no father, another male head of a household or senior male kin will ensure that by the time the boy is sixteen, he will be a thoroughly proficient fisherman. His pay is equal to that of the other fishermen and he has responsibilities commensurate with his size and strength. Using small craft they bring back lobster, crab, conch and fish from the reefs. These days they say spear fishing is easier, so the older man will row and hold the boat over the spot while the younger man, coming into his own, uses his strength to dive with the spear gun.

Even those who do not look to the sea for their living are fishermen. Often, on the broken piers jutting out, you will find a lone figure casting a throw-net made of a fine mesh fillet with lead weights fringing its circular edges. Those with a real skill throw the net wide open, so that your view of the sea's surface becomes criss-crossed through the diamond netting. If the timing is right, the net covers a shoal and the weights pull together, making a bag which imprisons the fish.

On the windward side of the small island of Carriacou, live the descendants of Scottish shipwrights brought down to the island by the planters to build their inter-island schooners. The fishing boats are often still built by hand. In Trinidad they work around a ribbed frame, for which the cedar tree is especially prized because its branches grow out from the trunk in an almost perfect shape for the ribs. The trees are carefully chosen and felled. One side of the log is then flattened and the shape of the boat drawn on to this surface. An *adze*, a kind of axe, is used to hollow out the trunk up to this line and to a depth of approximately 23 cm. The outside is then shaped and a keel fitted. Styles vary a little from one island to another, the different kind of waves and waters determining the shape. The launching in Carriacou is a fascinating ceremony for it is blessed by the priest and its safety in the waters insured by sacrificing a goat and a sheep, whose blood is sprinkled on the new deck. With much imbibing of the local jackiron – a lethal home brew of white rum – the big drum dance is performed while the men 'cutlash down' the boat, releasing it into the water with rhythmic strokes of their cutlasses, following the chant, 'stout boat, stout boat, stout boat', and the beat of the drums.

Each fisherman who works on the small reef craft is expected to provide his own boat and tackle, while his wife often works on the nets. It can take up to a month to make each one. Fish caught on the Atlantic coast of Grenada are landed right there on the beach; they clean them, cut them, but do not fillet or scale them. Then they hang them in the hot breezy air in long lines on wires. The flesh dries as the wind and sun catch it. The locals there swore by a dried grouper, an acquired taste I suspect. It would seem very similar to an account of a dish found in West Africa called *bomini*. Where he lived close to the sea, it was observed that the African enjoyed eating it very much. It consisted of dried fish, 'dried in the sun, without salt; stinking, they put it in a frying pan with Palm oil'.

In Grenada I enquired how they cooked the salted-dried fish. They said they roasted it as it was, straight on the barbecue. For how long? That remained in the wind. However, I imagine ten minutes each side would do it, but that explains not scaling it, for the juices are kept in the flesh and not lost. They then washed it thoroughly, removing the skin and bones and the salt, I presume. If any of the smoky flavour from the barbecue remained after that, it could be rather good. It was then served with a garnish of finely chopped onion rings, a few slices of avocado pear, and breadfruit with a few finely-chopped tomatoes and plenty of oil. I add, here, that if you used a very good extra virgin oil and nothing less, the dish would be excellent even without the smoky flavour.

If you have already lit a fire, the breadfruit is a very good addition to any barbecue. It can be mashed like potatoes, fried like chips and is especially good when peeled, sliced and served cold and dressed with olive oil. Pull out the central core and place it downwards in its skin into the coals, turning it regularly for an hour or so, until the knife slips into the centre easily.

The breadfruit was first discovered in Polynesia by Captain Cook and Joseph Banks, who returned to England with descriptions of a tree from which 'bread itself is gathered as a fruit'. The news eventually reached the ears of the West Indian planters and its value was recognized as another cheap source of food for their slaves as it bears fruit within three to six years. They petitioned George III to send an expedition to collect samples of the breadfruit, and so Captain Bligh was dispatched to Tahiti; his failure, because of the mutiny, is well known, but his second voyage was more successful, and he survived to return to Jamaica and St Vincent where to this day you can still see the tree he planted in 1793 in the botanical gardens. It is an immensely impressive tree and the dark glossy leaves stand out like great hands, so deeply are the seven or so fingers pinnately cut towards the centre. Against this hand the round fruit ripen and show up, lime green in the sunlight. They proliferate all over the tree and ripen in anything from sixty to ninety days.

The island of St Vincent had been captured from the French by the British in 1762 and grants of land had been made available throughout the islands. Planters came from Barbados, Nevis and Antigua to settle there. It was the descendant of a Scottish family, the Warners – who were granted lands in Bequia in 1763 – who built the first whaling station in 1875. The whales are now gone: many years can now pass without so much as a sighting. Only Aytheneal Oliverre, reputedly the last of the true whalers in the Western Hemisphere, remains. The seventy whales caught since 1958, he claims as his.

All that remains now is a mention on a map – 'whaling station ruins' – and the trace of a West Country accent undulating still in a few soft sounds left by those who came those generations ago. The people who once worked on the whaling boats usually lived on the Atlantic side where the whales would pass by. Here the sands are black, the grains worn fine from the boulders once belched out from the volcanic heart of the island. On these distant stretches of beach, the sighing of a forgotten world is thrown away unheard into the sea-misted air. Forlorn palms lean into the winds and the poverty of the dwellings is exaggerated by the cruel light from the metallic lustre of the black volcanic sand and the aluminium sheen from the sea.

Even when whaling was a flourishing business, it was a struggling existence for the men who worked on the boats. The whale boat owners not only owned the boats, but all the equipment too. It required great skill and courage working in those waters with only a harpoon in an open 8 m boat. The crewmen received a third-share of the whale meat, which they took home to their settlements and salted what they could not eat straight away. The owners shipped their part of the meat to the fish market in St Vincent, keeping control of the export of the much valued whale oil. It is still so today. On the rare occasion that a whale is caught, one-third goes to the boat owner, another third to the captain or harpooner, and the remainder to the crewmen.

When you do from time to time find whalemeat in the market, it is smoked black and looks forbidding. With a lot of soaking and coaxing it can be made edible. We were once offered such a dish by a couple who ran a rum shop in St Vincent, where much of the whaling used to be done. I was relieved it was not the whale's heart, which is claimed by locals as the real delicacy. It was a treat for them and an honour for us, since the smoked flavour persisted through the hours of cooking over an ancient coal pot blackened by generations of users. The strong white rum, with its scent of night's blossoms, was a welcome and necessary digestive for the dark fibrous meat, thoroughly oily and hard.

Whatever the hardships the men might have endured, they became extraordinarily skilled seamen. Having been used to fishing in traditional dugout canoes or square-sterned fishing boats, they had to learn to adapt and work on the open double-bowed sailboat modelled on the Nantucket whalers. The sailing skills for which they became famed gave them a new freedom to go further afield to fish, although they had to provide their own transport to do it.

During the first half of this century in Bequia, small-time fishermen managed to find their own markets in the nearby islands, especially St Vincent. Their small boats were able to cope with such short distances and local demand exceeded their supplies. Once the French traders moved in to buy for export, the planter-merchants saw their opportunity to expand and refitted their trading schooners with freezing equipment. Now most of the local fish is caught by them and sold direct to the French, leaving the small fisherman forced to work for one or other of the three descendants of planter families. This means joining their 'seine boats', for he must take what he can get. The boats hold a crew of seven and can carry nets of up to 914 m. He works entirely as they did in the old days, on the owners' terms and he cannot argue. Once again, the small man's success has been countered and the social differences increased.

There are considerable risks for the lone fishermen who venture out beyond the reef. Despite the images we all have today of calm white beaches and serene seas reflecting the changing blues of the Caribbean skies, the waters around and between the islands can be difficult and treacherous. On one side there is the agitated might of the Atlantic, breaking with relentless force; on the other, the smooth sheltered and unperturbed waters of the Caribbean protected by the reef. Where these waters meet between each island, there can be tremendous disturbances and dangerous currents.

For those who venture out too far there is always the chance that the reefs may catch them, or the treacherous currents may beguile the craft towards the Venezuelan waters. There are often intriguing accounts from survivors of such a happening, who come back with tales of engine failure, and many days being nervously spent swept away by the currents towards the South American mainland, before being picked up by a larger vessel.

Those who sail the boats know exactly which banks to head for. The names of the fish caught read like poetry: the *cacatois*, *cordonnier* – the Creole names for the parrotfish and rabbitfish – the *bourgeois*, coral trout, yellowtail and kingfish. When sprung by whatever means from the depths, they surpass the screaming jungle colours of tropical birds. Travellers by ship to the Indies have reported seeing between fifty and a thousand flying fish leap clear out of the water altogether. As if at some pre-arranged signal they decide to show off their slim silver-blue bodies in dazzling bypasses of up to 23 m.

'Flying fish, which surprised me very much,' recalled Gustavus, 'frequently fly across the ship and many of them fell onto the deck . . . the clouds appeared to me to be land, which disappeared as they passed along. This heightened my wonder and I was now persuaded more than ever that I was in another world and that everything about me was magic.'

Through December to June, flying fish are plentiful, especially around Barbados. The boats there are specially designed to catch the flying fish and are a fine sight, their shallow draughts resting lightly, like short bright, red and blue brush-strokes on the quiet green waters inside the reef. To catch the flying fish, palm fronds are ingeniously laid across the sea's surface: the fish rise out of the sea and are deceived into thinking the fronds are the land, where they could lay their eggs, and so they are trapped.

Filleting the fish itself is quite a skill. It does not surprise me at all that the deft cutting and boning by the women held fast in the memory of Aldous Huxley, who travelled through the region in the thirties. He wrote:

> In a back room behind a shop, lit by a dim oil lamp, a very old negress was sitting with her hat on, of course cleaning flying fish. Snick snick – off went the long fins, the tail, the head; another snick, out came the guts and, with a little manipulation, the backbone. The fish was dropped into the basket. An incredibly beautiful, pale brown girl was sitting beside her, sewing. The door behind them was open to the seas . . . the young woman so beautiful, with her face shining in the lamplight, as though illuminated from within, the old Negress, under her battered hat, black hands busy among the silvery fish.

In Barbados they have a fine blend of **seasonings for fish** which they pack into the seams once they have filleted them. They mince together onions, parsley, thyme, garlic and a little red seasoning pepper, combine the mixture with salt, black pepper and paprika to taste, and lime juice to blend. These ingredients are varied in amounts according to your taste, left for the flavour to develop, then rubbed carefully into the fillets to penetrate the flesh before frying or steaming. The locally much-appreciated kingfish lurks in the deeper waters beyond the reef. It is a very popular fish, for it has very few bones, and marries very well with a sauce made with chestnuts.

For **Kingfish with Chestnut Sauce** marinade four steaks in some fresh lime juice for 1–2 hours in the refrigerator. To prepare the sauce you will need 100–125 g (4 oz) of cooked and peeled chestnuts, 1 finely chopped spring onion, including the green stem, 2 tablespoons of finely chopped parsley, 1 crushed clove of garlic, 4 tablespoons of minced shallots or onions, 1 teaspoon of fresh lime juice, a pinch of black pepper, 2–3 drops of pepper sauce, 2 tablespoons of olive oil and salt to taste. While you barbecue the fish steaks, allowing five minutes each side and adding a few drops of oil and rock salt, chop half of the chestnuts very finely and the other half roughly. Sauté all the ingredients together for about ten minutes in the olive oil until the onion and garlic begin to turn a golden colour. Add the lime juice and the hot pepper sauce. Garnish the fish with watercress and serve the sauce separately.

These days the stocks of fish are becoming depleted around some islands, so the men often have to travel further than they used to. From Bequia they sail down to the Tobago keys where they camp out. On the way they may troll, pulling a line with live bait on it to catch migratory fish such as the tuna and cavalla, each man notching his fish in a particular way so there can be no argument when it comes to sharing out the catch. Most of the fish are sold to the French traders on the islands of Union and Canouan.

Once we talked with the fishermen returning with their catch, who explained to us with great relish and anticipation what a 'brof' (broth) was. When they have pulled the boat up on the beach, if the day has been long and hard, they do not go home, but light a fire there and then. Then they fill a large pot with sea water and drop in whatever fish they have caught, with some local vegetables such as plantain, sweet potatoes or yam. It looked and smelled delicious. One of the fishermen explained to me how the 'ole folk' used to improve the flavour of a soup or stew by dropping a piece of seasoning pork into the pot for a few minutes. They kept the fat pork, which could also have been smoked, hanging by a string over the stove or coal pot and would lower it when they felt the pot needed pepping up. The larger it was, the more often they would use it. If you have a small piece of salted meat or fish you could do the same when making a broth.

 To make a **Fish Broth** for four people you will need, and most fishmongers now can give you one, a head of a tropical *bourgeois* weighing 1–1.5 kg (2–3 lb), or a snapper, parrotfish or redfish. Then choose firm white fish only – such as swordfish, monk fish, halibut – and buy enough for four people. Try to make it a mixture. The remainder of the ingredients represent a temperate or northern alternative to the fresh vegetables you can get in the Caribbean. In terms of balancing the sweetness, I have used parsnips instead of

sweet potatoes. 1 teaspoon of grated ginger, 60 g (2 oz) of parsley, 60 g (2 oz) of chopped celery, 90 g (3 oz) of chopped carrots, 1 chopped spring onion (keep green tops for later), 500 g (1 lb) of very finely diced Spanish or other mild onions, 2–3 de-seeded and sliced up seasoning peppers, olive oil for frying, 1 glass of dry white wine, 1–2 tablespoons of rock salt, ½ teaspoon of black pepper, 1 head of garlic cut diagonally, 4–6 allspice berries, 1–2 small bay leaves, 1 tablespoon of curry powder, 120 g (4 oz) of turnips, 120 g (4 oz) of parsnips and 120 g (4 oz) of thinly chopped leeks. Put the fish head in a muslin bag. Fry the grated ginger, parsley, celery, carrots, spring onion, Spanish onion and seasoning peppers in olive oil until soft. Add a glass of dry white wine. Add the head and cover with water. Add the salt, pepper and garlic, allspice, bay or pimento leaf, curry powder, chopped turnips and parsnips. Bring to the boil and let it barely tremble for forty-five minutes, then skim off any scum, though with tropical heads there is usually very little. Add the leeks, green tops of the onions and the fish you have chosen. Simmer for another ten to fifteen minutes at the most. Watch carefully at this stage for the fish must be kept whole and only just cooked. Remove from the heat and take out the head. You can either remove the fish steaks and serve with some sautéd Caribbean vegetables, straining the stock and serving it first as a thin soup, or serve it altogether in large serving bowls.

When the fisherman's catch includes some red snapper, we often barbecue it in the following way on the beach. It takes almost no preparation and is very easy to do.

 For **Barbecued Red Snapper** cut off the snapper's head, slice along the length of its stomach and remove the contents, keeping the liver. Bury the guts immediately, deep in the sand away from your picnic, wash the fish in the sea, cut through the backbone so that you have the fish in two pieces. You will notice I did not say scale; this is why your job is so easy and the flesh remains unimaginably juicy and succulent. Place the two sides of the fish flat between the wire fish holders and place scale-side down over the charcoal which by now should be hot and glowing red. Allow five minutes each side. Serve on fresh banana leaves with a squeeze of freshly picked lime. If we drive through a plantation on our way to the beach we ask for banana leaves and limes, which people are always glad to give us.

The tourist taste is very much for the redfish and snapper, so the fishermen can charge considerable prices for these. It is possible now to buy good fresh snapper in Europe and America. In England, Billingsgate market always has good supplies, mostly flown in the day before from the Seychelles. They should come in on ice; however, be sure that they were gutted before being frozen.

If you should ever have to clean a tropical fish, wear rubber gloves for the spines can be lethally sharp and in the tropics they can easily infect you. Cut off all the fins along the back and stomach of the snapper, then cut from the middle of the stomach up through the mouth. Grasp the red gills each side of the cheeks and pull firmly; the stomach and guts should come away with them. With a very sharp knife, hold the tail firmly, and pressing the blade down and forward towards the head, lift the scales off. Wash the inside free of any blood, but not the outside if you can avoid it. Rub inside and out with the oil, lime juice, garlic, pepper and salt, and leave there for two to three hours.

To cook **Red Snapper in a Court Bouillon,** West Indian style, you will need a snapper large enough for three people, olive oil, black pepper, lime or lemon juice, garlic and salt. To make the bouillon you will need 600 ml (1 pint) of water, 2–3 tablespoons of lemon or lime juice, 1 teaspoon of black pepper, 1 small very finely chopped shallot, 1 clove of crushed garlic, 1 dessertspoon of soy sauce, 1 tablespoon of chopped tomato (leave the skin on), 2 tablespoons of chopped parsley, 2 pimento and nutmeg or bay leaves. Simmer gently all the court bouillon ingredients with the juices that have developed in the snapper marinade for ten to fifteen minutes; lower the snapper into the pan. Cover with a lid or foil and cook for fifteen minutes on each side. Remove the fish to a serving dish and reduce the stock to half; add a knob of butter and cook for a few minutes more, or until it has melted and stir well, then adjust the seasoning with more salt or lemon if needed. Serve the fish sprinkled with parsley and the sauce separately.

Often in the Windward Islands the Atlantic coasts are not developed for tourists. The land behind the strand of coral often lies lower than sea-level and is dense with coconut trees. Few people would choose to live here. The odd animal might be tethered and left in lonely contemplation and the land crab digs deep into the ground. The beaches remain in a more natural and wildly beautiful state, roughened by the force of the Atlantic. The hot white sand is finely graded from the corals of the deep, through white to beige to pink, softly crushed together in a million splintered fractions. Out beyond the reefs, often some hundred metres off shore, the Atlantic waves meet their first opposition after travelling across 8,000 kilometres of open sea. They can be heard orchestrating the breaking waves with a constant dull roar; the sound is deeply soothing.

On some of the beaches you may find shacks or small buildings where the Caribbean fishermen own their cooperatives. These now largely sell lobsters to the American markets, an iniquitous practice since it is only the tails that are wanted. However, the advantage is that on remote beaches you may find they are just landing their catch, and be able to pick up the remains. It was a Frenchman who showed me how to take the coral – the lobster's red eggs – wash it in the sea and eat it there and then with a little lime juice freshly squeezed on to it. It is quite a sensational rich experience. You could alternatively travel with a small pan, light a fire and bring approximately 600 ml of sea water to the boil. Whatever claws or bits from the head of the lobster you have been fortunate enough to scavenge, poach very gently in the barely trembling sea water for up to ten minutes, depending on how well cooked you like your lobster meat to be. I like it barely cooked, so I allow no more than three to four minutes.

If you can, buy a whole lobster from the fisherman, collecting a coconut and callaloo leaves on your way home. Callaloo, or dasheen, taro or cocoyam, as it can be called in different places by different peoples, is a root crop; some roast, bake or boil the corms, or even make it into *fou-fou*, others blanch the young shoots and eat them as they would asparagus. In Trinidad especially, it is the leaves that are sought after. Interestingly it was most probably propagated by flies, who spread it from China to Japan; it was next seen in Africa by Pliny when he visited Egypt in AD 23–79; and later reached the rain forests on the Guinea coast, from where it travelled to the West Indies to help feed the slaves.

The plants like to grow in long rows, following the drains or kitchen outflows in obedient lines, for they need plenty of water. The new yellow-green leaves shoot up rolling inward at the apex; as they grow, they unfurl into the shape of elephants' ears, softly velutinous and becoming a darker green as the leaves age. It has been said that the African marriage of the flavours of the callaloo leaf with seafood is one of the most inspired of dishes in the entire repertoire of Caribbean cuisine. Certainly it makes an excellent starter. Choose fresh young leaves.

For **Lobster Callaloo** allow a 500 g (1 lb) lobster for two people. Clean it carefully. Have ready 125 g (¼ lb) of salt beef, 600 ml (1 pint) of coconut milk, 8–10 callaloo or spinach leaves, half a very finely chopped large onion and 3 seasoning peppers, 1 spring onion, coconut oil for frying, and 4–5 okra, finely chopped into rings. The salt beef should be finely diced and brought to the boil, then simmered in 300 ml (½ pint) of the coconut milk until soft. It should be ready by the time you have prepared the rest of the ingredients. So meanwhile heat the oil and add the onions, seasoning peppers and spring onion. When the onions have just turned brown cut the lobster tail in two down the middle of the back and add it, plus the cracked claws. Turn thoroughly in the mixture until it changes colour and add the okra and callaloo. Pour over the coconut milk, add the beef and the coconut milk it was cooked in. Put on a lid and simmer gently for twenty minutes. It is really delicious.

Today the inherited passionate attachment to the sea and its bounty is undiminished. There have been many evenings that we have spent in the local rum shop perched on crocus bags filled with flour, sitting there quietly listening and watching the scene as groups of people come and go. Some come early to shop for essentials to make up a meal for that evening. Today, throughout the English-speaking Caribbean, in the local rum shops and small food shops you will see lists of foodstuffs printed on fading posters by the door for all to see, for the Government regularly dictates the cost of each item, such as flour, kerosene, candles and bully beef.

Later the fishermen, having sold their day's catch locally, will gather and order an eighth or *petite* of rum, sometimes white, sometimes red. (A gill is a quarter of a pint, and a little more is a 'big gill'.)

As the evening progresses and the talk becomes more animated, the owner may bring out small bowls of food, perhaps some souse made from conch or 'lambie' as it is called there, to take up the rum. The profiles of well-fed men become beautifully lit and stand out sombrely against the warm wood-slatted walls. With tongues oiled and stomachs heated with the fire of the peppers in the souse, the atmosphere becomes cosy and the black night held at bay. Talk is usually about the difficulties of making a dollar by fishing alone. 'Only a few years ago, we was able to manage from my fishin, now my wife has to sharecrop,' complains a fisherman and continues: 'I have to travel down to the cays and it ain't fair to leave my wife for so long.' Others say that working on the seine is not much better either, for the catch is small and the owner does not even have the heart to help. 'Most of us we are trying for to feed we family and he ain't care.' Others try to remain, or fish with a friend.

One night I spoke to a fisherman and his companion, both descendants of the African who knew broader beaches 'where the coughing of lions was dumbed by the breakers,' as Derek Walcott described it. He sighed with regret at not having planned to fish that night. 'I jealous the sea,' he said to me. They stood together that black-moon night, guarding their dreams of the sea, their mistress, until the next trip.

UNSEASONED ÉMIGRÉS

Portugalers with us have truth in hand:
Whose Marchandy commeth much into England.
They bene our frendes wyth there commoditez,
And wee English passen into there Countrees.

Anon

In 1846 the first group of Portuguese immigrants arrived in Trinidad, at Port of Spain, to be transported to the sugar estates in Caroni. There is very little left by way of records to give us a detailed account of the Portuguese way of life in the island, but events are clear enough from the basic facts. 'Few are they who are left to tell their tale of woe . . .', ran a desperate petition to the Governor of Trinidad by the Portuguese, describing how their countrymen had been reduced to only one-third of their original number; 'The rest have fallen victims to the unhealthiness of the climate or to the cruelties of the slavery system to which we, equally with the unfortunate blacks, have been subjected to.'

Today there is nothing to commemorate the dead. The swamps near Caroni, where the white, red and black mangrove trees lower their roots into the brackish water in a forbidding web of cross hatching, keep their secrets. It is an area that covers over 5,000 hectares of tidal lagoons and green marshlands. At dusk the sky can darken and streak as if with a sudden sunset, when as many as 12,000 scarlet ibis lower their wings and rest like sheets of flame fanning upward from the green branches of the mangrove trees. The first Portuguese could not have failed to see this sight and wonder at it.

The Portuguese had been brought to the island from Madeira to replace the African after emancipation. The British Government finally had to accept that the African would no longer work on the estates on the terms that the planter and Government wanted, and labour was needed to plant the cocoa which was becoming an ever more valuable crop to the British planter.

The search had begun for an alternative pool of labour to work on the estates. Speeches were made in Parliament about the need for a white middle class of farmers who would have a civilizing effect on the ex-slaves, and contribute their invaluable knowledge of husbandry and stabilize society. Europeans, it was said, could work in the new cocoa estates safely, because the work would be more shaded from the sun and less arduous than in the sugar-cane fields.

The people to whom the British looked were the Portuguese. It was a curious turning of the tables. Portugal had played a powerful role in the discovery of the New World: was it not Vasco de Gama who discovered the true Indies in 1498 and the Portuguese who had kept a stranglehold on the spice trade? The Governor of Trinidad had allowed the Portuguese to hold concessions and cultivate the land with the Amerindians as a labour force, until the King of Spain ordered them out. Even after that they had remained, keeping their monopoly on the cocoa and shipping it back to Europe.

Besides this, Portuguese and Plantagenet blood had been fused in the fourteenth century. Trade between the two countries flourished and Newfoundland salted cod was bartered for salt, fruit, honey, cork and wine. So great was the English liking for the wine called Red Portugal that English coopers were sent to teach the Portuguese how to make the casks to store and transport it. Madeiran wine was exceedingly fashionable in England too, until the 1840s when port became more popular instead. This especially affected the Madeirans who relied heavily on exporting it to England.

Now they returned as indentured labourers under three to five year contracts. The majority came from the Madeiran archipelago, where years of famine and religious persecution made the chance to escape seem a heaven-sent opportunity. By 1855 over 40,000 people had left Madeira for the West Indian estates. Large numbers were willing to go out to Trinidad and Guyana, and a few smaller groups also left for Grenada and Jamaica.

In theory they were in a much better position than the African. It was no longer considered ethical to chain them down; wages and return passage had to be paid, as well as the fees to the recruiting agent. The British Government also stipulated that they should not work in the sugar fields. Yet in other ways their position was not so very different from that of the African. Significantly, they were not even considered to be white.

Amongst those who left Madeira for the Caribbean were the Mendes family, who fled across the Atlantic in 1836 in open fishing boats, finally landing in Trinidad. In this century a descendant of that same family, who now lives in Barbados, has written an account of the 'forces which gathered strength and exploded into violence against my ancestors more than a quarter and a half centuries ago'. Apparently a missionary zealot from Scotland, who had been ordered by his doctor to take the air in Madeira, felt called on by his destiny to a 'furious exercise of proselytising' to the Madeirans. Mass conversions followed. In response Catholic mobs, inflamed by the priests, looted and destroyed the houses and possessions of an already impoverished people.

Tragically, many had made the hazardous journey – both Catholics and converts – only to find themselves in an even more miserable plight. Whatever the conditions the British Government had laid out in the terms of the recruitment, the Portuguese were poorly housed, ill-fed and overworked. Heartbreaking petitions were drawn up by the immigrants. 'Collect us all up and send us home,' they pleaded, 'Men and women have suffered the greatest misery and oppression on the several estates where they have been forced to work beyond their strength by coercion of the whip and without proper shelter at night or food by day.' Mendes wrote: 'The barracks were inhospitable and the attitude of the Scottish overseers, brutal . . . the humidity within the green shade of the cocoa trees was a menace to health.'

These harsh realities make a bitter contrast with an idealized description by Yseult Bridges, daughter of an English estate owner living at Glenside in Trinidad. Accompanying her father to whichever part of the estate was being worked that day, was, she wrote, 'a happy blend of duty and pleasure'.

Under the misty shade of the cocoa trees, which the rising sun was piercing with quivering golden spears, the air was moist and cool . . . the cocoa-lilies, with petals like long satin streamers, were drenching the air with perfume . . . Squirrels, insects, birds and deer were all gratefully taking in the warmth of the early morning sun . . . High above this scene spread the branches of the mountain Immortelle, a giant of a tree, its branches aflame with orange blossoms in the spring, introduced and planted especially to give shade to the Cocoa. Its splendour would attract butterflies of staggering beauty – the Emperor (Morpho), a brilliant blue, the Mortbleu, purple and saffire – fluttered with slow wing beats in seemingly aimless indolence.

Below, the scene would have been far from indolent. Men and women were fully engaged in the many processes of harvesting and preparing the cocoa pods for export. The cocoa beans do not all ripen at once on the same tree, but can be seen in all stages of ripeness and colours, from deep green to maroon and gold, growing straight out of the trunks and branches. A good cocoa bean should be clean and a rich mahogany colour. When ripe the hard elongated ribbed shell should be brittle and the seeds easily lifted out. There were usually two harvests a year with the odd pickings in-between. The workers were equipped with cutlasses and goulettes, which were long poles with blades attached and were used to cut the stout stems that held the ripe cocoa pods to the trees. Pruning the trees was a constant operation as was the 'brushing' of the undergrowth. At the same time the pods would be gathered up and sliced open. The women squatted around the great heaps of opened pods and scooped out the slimy beans, which taste delicious and fruity, throwing them into panniers made from local liana vines.

The English shipped out almost every beast of burden that they thought would help with the variety of labouring tasks to be done on the estates. They had even brought the camel to Barbados in the sixteenth century to do the work horses could not manage, for it could carry up to 700 kg in weight of hogsheads containing sugar, wine, beer and vinegar. But invaluable as they were, they did not give them the right diet and they died out. The donkey, and most useful of all, the mule, came later and are still used a great deal in country regions today. For the cocoa operation they used donkeys; lines of them stood in a sun-drowsed state while the panniers were filled, then they carried the laden panniers to the sweating boxes.

Here the beans were left for approximately a week in a dark box until they had turned brown. They were then dried in the sun to remove the slime. Now they were ready to be 'danced' by the men with their bare feet, to polish the seeds a gleaming mahogany. They writhed their bodies to music strummed by a Negro on the Spanish quatro, a small four-stringed guitar. He also kept a wary eye on any threatening rain clouds; even as he shouted out the warning, the rain would start to fall and the men would have to work furiously to pull together the two halves of the massive sliding wooden roofs which ran in and out on rails.

Many of these rails have still not succumbed to the ravages of tropical weather and survive in the countryside. Beside them wooden supports for the sliding roof are destructively embraced by the mauve-pink star-like flowers of the congea, a rapacious orchid vine, and the toughened coral vine which tumbles down with deceptively delicate strings and showers of small pink hearts.

Of those Madeirans who survived the rigours of work on the plantations, both press and planter noted that they gave 'great satisfaction to their employers'. It was hardly surprising. After all, these people had coerced eight hundred odd square kilometres of mountainous volcanic rock into fruitful production.

Madeira's climate was, in its own way, as tortuous as that of the tropics: scorching days were followed by freezing nights. The terrain was equally uncompromising. Richard Ligon, whose ship had called there, wrote that it was 'so rocky and mountainous, and the ground so miserably burnt by the sun, as we could perceive no part of either hill or valley, that had the least appearance of green . . . instead of that fresh and lively green, other countries put on at this time of year, these were apparell'd with russets or at best rhyliamorts.'

Working and planting the soil in these barren cones of lava, rising sheer and stark from the Atlantic, must have been very hard indeed. When the island was first settled in the fifteenth century, terraces were niched by hand into the rock and cultivated. The water supply to keep the produce irrigated had to be brought down from the high central plateau in water courses that were also hewn by hand. Even the churches were carved from the rock itself. Only with enormous industry had the islands been turned into the fecund paradise with an abundance of fruits and flowers admired by travellers and visitors.

Some seamen mentioned by Ligon had described the islands as 'exceedingly fruitful and pleasant, abounding with all sorts of excellent fruits, corn, wine, oil and the best sugars'. He told of cattle, sheep, goats, hogs and poultry of all sorts.

Many English ships passed by and stopped on their way to the West Indies to take on fresh supplies for the rest of the journey and the *vino tinto* – tainted with a tint – 'though they assure tis the natural grape and "limed" as a preservative against the excessive heat of the West Indies'. The hospitality they received tells us much about the style of living the Madeirans enjoyed. According to Ligon and others, the kitchens had earthen floors, cobwebs for hangings, and frying pans and griddles for pictures. Ligon compared them to the 'meanest Inn upon the London Way'. 'But,' he added, 'they eat well.'

In other accounts one reads so much about the excellence of the fruit, meat and fish in this region that there can be no doubt that the Madeirans, poor as they might be, were in a blessed position by contrast with those at home in Portugal. They could exploit the sea around them, and the proximity to Africa gave them a more regular supply and variety of fruit, such as oranges and lemons. Ligon's ship's company were presented with different dishes of fruits, which then must have seemed truly exotic. 'Plantine, Bonanos, Guavers, Prickled pears and Custard apples' were served with red sack to refresh the men in the heat of the day.

In this sense Madeiran cuisine was Atlantic rather than Mediterranean in origin, once again influenced by its proximity to the African coast. The Portuguese were familiar with *cou-cou* and shared the art of kebabing, for example. The Portuguese threaded their pieces of meat on sticks of green laurel, marinading it first in wine, garlic, black pepper and olive oil; the Africans rubbed their meat with allspice and herbs and laid it on freshly cut pimento sticks. I use fillet of lamb for either version, marinading for twenty-four hours and barbecuing over glowing charcoal. Plantains boiled in their skins, sliced thinly lengthways and finished off on the barbecue for two to three minutes are a good accompaniment.

Nonetheless, there are Mediterranean echoes underlying this. Like their forebears and family in Portugal, Madeirans were a seafaring people, vine growers and onion planters: the influence these activities had on their cuisine was strongly marked. At home the onion planters had always supplied enormous quantities of onions, which were cooked in great shallow earthenware dishes over the fires until they turned to a pulp. Garlic and white wine would be added for a sauce known as *rofogada*.

The best sort of saltwater fish abounded. Ligon wrote of the romance upon seeing a weary sea hawk resting upon the back of a sleeping turtle: 'There, they mute, prune and oil their feathers . . . for some of those turtles are a yard broad in the back: we took one with our long boat . . . the whole body afforded all the gentlemen and officers of the ship a very plentiful meal and was the best meat we tasted.' In these same waters they saw the loggerhead, green and hawkesbill turtle of which the latter was 'the best'. The sailors also pulled in 'dolphin', which they dressed and served with wine, spices and sweet herbs. By this, they probably meant the dorado, a fish of a glorious sweetness of flesh and a skin marked with swathes of patternless blue and gold, like the movement of oil on water.

Mullet is a good alternative to the dorado in the North, as I find that there are hints of tropical fish tastes in the slightly muddy quality that it has. Mullet does freeze quite well for a week or so, but choose fish that are fresh. Ask the fishmonger first.

I have adapted this method when preparing mullet. If you ask the fishmonger to give you the livers when he has cleaned the fish and after you have cooked them, sieve them into the sauce with an addition of some wine vinegar, you will have a remarkably good and unusual sauce. For **Mullet** for four people allow one fish per person and the livers, 1 tablespoon each of unsalted butter and water to each liver that you use, 1 large Spanish onion, 50 ml (2 fl oz) of good extra virgin olive oil, 50 ml (2 fl oz) of dry white wine, 2 cloves of crushed garlic, salt and pepper to taste and a quarter of a teaspoon of sugar, the juice of half a lemon, 5 tomatoes, 2 tablespoons of red maille wine vinegar and 1 tablespoon of parsley. Fry the finely sliced onion in the oil for twenty to thirty minutes until completely soft, with the lid on. Now raise the heat to high and add the wine very slowly, so as not to seize the onions. Reduce by two-thirds then add the garlic, salt and pepper and sugar to taste. Mash the livers with a little salt to taste to a pulp and fry in the unsalted butter and water. Let it melt, not boil, then add the lemon juice, and sieve. Now sieve the tomatoes after you have removed the skins by dropping them into boiling water for a few minutes. Pour them over the bottom of an earthenware dish and lay the fish across the tomatoes. Pour a little extra olive oil over the fish to keep it moist, mix the livers into the onion and wine mixture and pour over the fish. Bake for fifteen minutes, then turn carefully using a spatula. Pour the vinegar over the fish and bake for another five minutes. Serve with a sprinkling of finely chopped parsley.

There are few details of the Portuguese living conditions in the West Indies, but those we do have suggest a pitifully poor quality of life by contrast with that the Madeirans had left behind. In the early days on the estate they would undoubtedly have made **milho frito** for breakfast, a very old Madeiran dish and very cheap to make. It is also extremely heavy and filling: 500 g (1 lb) of meal flour and some salt is mixed with 1.5 litres (2½ pints) of water, 30 g (1 oz) of heated lard and 30 g (1 oz) of lard, to make a thick paste. This is left overnight, then cut into strips and fried in hot olive oil. Perhaps they washed it down with **cocoa tea**, which was a very basic drink that is still prepared by people in the country areas of the islands. They simply take a little of the dried cocoa and pound it into a small round cake to store it. When the time comes to make a drink from it, they light the coal pot and place a pot or tin over it, in which they bring some cold water to the boil with a stick of cinnamon to flavour. Then they grate the cocoa cake into it until the water is sufficiently strong with the taste of it and sweeten it with condensed milk. In the past, local honey from the estate hives or sugar from the curing house could have been used for sweetening.

It must have been extraordinary for the Africans, who had always been at the bottom of the pile, to see the Portuguese struggling as they had done. From the moment of their arrival in the islands, they worked side by side with less friction or tension between them than was the case with the groups who were brought in later to replace them on the estates.

Alongside this, there was a basic marriage of their cooking styles. Naipaul wrote of the 'Portuguese stew of tomatoes, in which anything might be done, the Negro way with yams, plantain and breadfruit'.

 Tomato Sauce on Cassava is a delicious combination that makes a very good cold starter. If cassava is not available, substitute yam. Allow 75–125 g (3–4 oz) of cassava, after peeling, per person, scrape it under running cold water, then put it into cold water and bring to the boil and simmer until tender – approximately twenty minutes. Test to see if it is done as you would an ordinary potato and slice thinly in lengthways strips. Allow to cool. Meanwhile make the dressing. For four servings you will need 1 medium Spanish or other mild onion sliced to transparent thinness, 2 crushed cloves of garlic, 2 tablespoons of extra virgin olive oil, 50 g (2 oz) of unsalted butter, 1 medium green pepper and half a stick of celery very thinly sliced,

500 g (1 lb) of well-chopped tomatoes, black pepper and salt to taste, 1 tablespoon of paprika, 1 teaspoon of Worcester sauce, 1 tablespoon of tomato paste, 1 tablespoon of chopped West Indian thyme or 2–3 sprigs. Fry the onions and garlic in the oil and butter until soft. Without stirring, lay the pepper and celery on top and cover with a lid until they are also softened. Arrange the chopped tomatoes across the mixture. Again, do not stir and cook for another ten minutes. Add all the remaining ingredients and mix gently into a pulp with a pestle, simmering for a further twenty minutes until the oil begins to separate. Let it get cold, then dress the sliced sticks of cassava with it.

The following two recipes show the same creole marriage of flavours. The tripe and pig's foot needed for this first recipe would have been cheap enough, but not so easy to obtain since whenever an animal was slaughtered the competition for the offal and extremities was keen indeed. The chorizo was imported.

For **Tripe stewed with Pig's Foot and Chorizo** for four people you will need 1 pig's foot cut into four pieces and soaked in salt water for an hour, then thoroughly washed. Buy 1 kg (2 lbs) of washed and ready prepared tripe. Both must now be marinaded in a large bowl overnight in the refrigerator. Cut up the tripe into 5 cm (1 inch) square pieces. Pour over them 175 ml (6 fl oz) of white rum, 2 tablespoons of olive oil, 2 tablespoons of lemon juice, 2 crushed cloves of garlic, 1 finely diced onion and a dust of fresh black pepper. Next day drain off the marinade and discard. To cook the main bulk of the dish you will need 150–175 ml (4–6 fl oz) of good virgin olive oil, 2 tablespoons of fresh chopped parsley and celery, 4–5 small diced carrots, 1 head of garlic cut diagonally, 3 chopped tomatoes, black pepper to taste, 1 hot chilli de-seeded, 1 bay or pimento leaf, 175–250 ml (6–8 oz) of chorizo, a handful of chopped leeks, 8–10 freshly ground allspice berries and 75 g (3 oz) of salted pork. Fry the tripe in the olive oil, keeping the heat fairly high until it turns a good golden colour, then add the pig's foot and parsley, celery, carrots, garlic, black pepper, onions. Cook on a lower heat with a lid on until the vegetables are softened. Add all the remaining ingredients except the pork. Stir well and cook for another ten minutes or longer until you see the juices are sweated out. Only then will you see how much water to add so that the ingredients are properly covered. Add the chopped up salt pork and cook slowly for another two and a half hours.

The second recipe, for oxtail, marries red wine with hot bird peppers. In England in 1758, Sarah Phillips wrote of the standard rough-and-ready approach to cutting up meat which has influenced the butchers in the Caribbean to this day: 'Hack it with a knife and rip open the belly.' Today the cutlash still serves for all the operations involved in butchering an animal, so always wash the meat and look carefully for splinters of bone.

For **Oxtail in Red Wine with Hot Bird Peppers** for three to four people you will need 750 g (1½ lbs) of oxtail, coconut oil for frying, 1 bird pepper, 2 medium onions, 1 tablespoon of chopped celery, 2 seasoning peppers, a whole head of garlic, salt and black pepper to taste, 120 ml (4 fl oz) of tomato ketchup, 120 ml (4 fl oz) of good red wine and 120 ml (4 fl oz) of water. Dry the pieces of oxtail and brown in the coconut oil with the bird pepper, taking great care that it does not burst. Add the finely chopped onion, celery, and seasoning peppers and head of garlic cut in half, add salt and pepper to taste. When these have all softened, push the ingredients around the edge of the pot to make a well and add the tomato sauce. Let it bubble, then stir to amalgamate. Add the red wine and allow it to bubble also – then stir altogether and simmer for five minutes. Add the water and stir. Cook for two hours, with a good lid on. Do not forget to remove the bird pepper.

This is simply delicious served with **Mashed Breadfruit**. While the oxtail is cooking, put a ripe breadfruit upside down in a moderately heated oven, resting it on a rack with a tray beneath, having taken its stalk off – for reasons best known to my advisor in the village. Bake it for one and a half to two hours in a moderate oven. Peel when it has cooled enough. Allow 90 g (3 oz) per person and mash with copious amounts of butter, milk and salt, as you would mashed potatoes. I must say that it makes all the difference if you put the breadfruit through the sieve. Painstaking though this is, it lightens it considerably. They use evaporated milk in the Caribbean and that is an improvement also.

One of the great staples of Portuguese and Madeiran cooking was, and still is, *bacalao* – salt-cod. Much of the winter diet in Portugal had depended on the boats surviving the arduous trip to Newfoundland. Each winter the fleet would assemble in the Tagus river and would sail through treacherous Northern Atlantic seas to the Grand Banks off Newfoundland to bring back the much valued cod. The dangers the men endured during those dark days when it hardly got light were extraordinary. They would leave the safety of their ships and fish from a small corracle called a *doris*, which held two men. On the return journey the cod was slit open, cleaned and salted. No matter what the winter seas were like, or the difficulties of organizing sail and oar, the salting had to be done. This especially applied to the herring whose fatty oils would quickly turn rancid within twenty-four hours of pulling in the catch.

In the fifteenth and sixteenth centuries the fleet would return to the Portuguese ports and supply the ships that were about to make the long journey to the New World with salted cod. Today the fleet follows the same routes, and there is a regular interchange of rum and salted cod between Newfoundland and the West Indies. In those intervening years salted cod has become an integral part of Caribbean cuisine.

According to Mendes, it was part of the everyday diet on the cocoa estates. Easy to keep, easy to prepare, it must have been a godsend to the exhausted cocoa workers, who perhaps did not always have organized facilities. At worst it could be roasted as it was. 'Now mind your charcoal fire is quite clear and red when you grill it', was the advice of one African woman. Perfect advice it was too. They would have laid the fillets of unsoaked, salted fish on the *fogareiro* – the Portuguese equivalent of the African's coal pot – grilled it for a few minutes each side and eaten it with traditional unleavened bread and a rough red wine. It was food for the very poor, and probably very salty to our tastes, but after sweating in the fields under the tropical sun, the salt must undoubtedly have been both welcome and very necessary. With a little embellishment, the same grilled salt-cod, but desalinated first for most people's tastes, is delicious as a cold hors-d'oeuvre.

 For **Grilled Salt-Cod** you will need a good quality fish. Soak it for twenty-four hours, changing the water once or twice – or more depending on the thickness of the fillets – then roast it over the charcoal. Let it cool, skin and remove the bones and dress it with good olive oil and a squeeze of fresh lime juice. You now have something special. I like to serve this cold with slices of plain avocado, or either hot or cold, dressed with a fresh tomato and wine sauce finished off with a little chopped coriander and fried strips of plantain.

Judging how to prepare saltfish depends on a knowledge of the fish itself. If it is old when it is caught, it will be tough no matter what you do to it; also the cut is very important. The cod meat packaged for the West Indian and English market tends to be the darker flesh with plenty of bone, and often smells stronger (they sometimes try to pass off coley or worse as cod, so check the package carefully). I use this for flavouring soups and stews. If you have a choice, ask for a piece near the end with some of the tail to increase the glutinous texture of the sauce. On the other hand, if the *bacalao* is for a cold hors-d'oeuvre buy thick steaks near the head from the Spanish, Portuguese or Italian grocers, who are usually careful to sell you good-quality fish. For such dishes I usually allow 125 g (4 oz) per person.

You will need to soak the salt-cod for almost all recipes, the length of time depending on the degree of saltiness. Do not guess: keep tasting unless you are absolutely sure of the fish. The length of time can be between twelve and thirty-six hours, and you will need to change the water two to three times at least. If you are in a desperate hurry and are using a cheap cut of fish, pour over plenty of boiling water and leave for an hour. Taste, and if necessary repeat. I do not really recommend this last method.

To this day the Portuguese settler in the West Indies will let the warmth of his memories of eating *bacalao* suffuse his features in a flush of nostalgia. The following recipe is based on a Portuguese method, with the additional use of red hot pepper.

For **Salt-cod Steaks in Peppered Olive Oil** for two people take 2 salt-cod steaks, 50 ml (2–3 fl oz) of a delicately flavoured (not heavy) olive oil, 2 sliced cloves of garlic, 1 small red chilli pepper and the juice of approximately half a fresh lime. Put your oil and de-seeded red pepper into a small saucepan. Heat the oil slowly for ten minutes, allowing the heat of the pepper to suffuse the oil, then remove it or it will be too hot – there should only be a hint. Add your steaks (the oil should come half way up their sides) and the garlic. Cook for thirty minutes at a very slow bubble. Squeeze in the fresh lime juice, allow to cool and serve as a cold starter with plain sliced boiled green bananas, which offset the cod very well, if somewhat unusually.

In the islands callaloo and *bacalao* are married in an excellent soup. In the following recipe the use of a small piece of saltfish or meat is merely a flavouring device. Spinach is a good substitute for the callaloo.

For smoked or salted flavoured **Callaloo Soup** for four people chop 500 g (1 lb) of washed spinach or callaloo leaf. Have ready 75–100 g (3–4 oz) of finely chopped saltfish or smoked meat such as bacon or ham, 600 ml (1 pint) of coconut milk, 2 tablespoons of olive oil, 25 g (1 oz) of unsalted butter, a pinch of dried thyme, black pepper, a few drops of pepper sauce, 2 small onions, 1 crushed clove of garlic and 2 tablespoons of good thick cream. Melt the butter and oil together quite gently and fry the saltfish or meat for five minutes. Add the very finely diced onion and garlic and cook until soft and melting away. Put a lid on to help the mixture to sweat. Having washed the spinach thoroughly, cook half the amount of the leaves for a few minutes in the water that adheres to the leaves. For the remaining spinach, shake off the excess water and add to the saltfish or meat, stir well and cook gently until soft. Put in a blender with the coconut milk and blend. Sieve the rest of the spinach, then mix the two together in a larger pot, adding the thyme, black pepper and pepper sauce. Without boiling, add the cream if you want to enrich it at the end, just letting it warm through.

Mendes wrote: 'Some of my forebears were fisher-folk who had become as familiar with the Atlantic, as with the wooded mountains and lush valleys of their fertile land [of Madeira] and would have been very much accustomed to handling and preparing fish of all kinds.' The swamp waters of southern Trinidad would have provided the Madeirans with a rich source of fresh fish, such as the mangrove snapper and the grouper, which has been known to weigh up to 45 kg. Grouper is a superb fish, if treated simply; try just barbecuing it.

For **Barbecued Grouper** buy enough fish for four people. Have it cleaned but not scaled, and do not let the fishmonger clean it under running water for all the flavour of the sea and flesh is lost. Cut off the head and cut the fish in half lengthways. Wipe only the inside clean. When the coals are glowing red hot, rub the flesh inside gently with salt, black pepper, olive oil and some lime juice. Place in a wire fish holder and put the scaly side to the heat for approximately ten to fifteen minutes. It is better and the flesh is juicier if underdone.

Those same swamp waters would have provided a plentiful amount of blue crab for the Portuguese dish called *santola no carro*, meaning crab in a carriage, which is a mixture of crab meat fried in onions and breadcrumbs with a few drops of *piri piri*, or hot pepper sauce. Since the peppers needed for the sauce and dish were found everywhere in the Caribbean, it is hardly surprising that they are used in many Caribbean dishes today.

To make **Piri Piri** take 2 chilli peppers. Choose the red variety for they contrast beautifully against the engine-oil green of the extra virgin olive oil, the yellow zest of a lemon, and the darker ash green of a pimento or bay leaf. Put them all into a jar with a good-fitting lid and leave on the boiler or radiator for two to three weeks. The longer you keep the *piri piri* the hotter it will get, so that it would be a good idea to remove the chillies after two to three months. Be sure that there are no blemishes on the chillies or they will spoil. A few drops will enhance almost all West Indian dishes, especially fish.

The Madeirans must also have looked to the sea for fish, catching whatever was in season at the time. Shark comes close inshore at certain times of the year when it is breeding and would have been easy to catch. Shark is very much underused and if seasoned beforehand is comparable with the best tropical fish.

 For **Barbecued Shark Steaks** have the shark meat skinned and cut into suitable-sized steaks. Then marinade in fresh lime juice, salt and black pepper and two to three drops of the *piri piri* for two days in the refrigerator. Put the steaks between a wire rack and place over the hot coals, close enough to the heat to let the lines of the wires mark the flesh in attractive brown stripes. As they are cooking, sprinkle a little rock salt and olive oil on each side. Cook for ten minutes each side. They are very good simply served with grated carrots that have been lightly dressed with a mixture of clear honey, lime juice to taste and olive oil.

In the West Indies today, they say the flesh of the shark is 'too fresh' when it is just caught, so it must be very carefully prepared indeed. However, if you are buying it as an imported fish this is not a problem. It is good to serve it as a starter.

 For **Shark Nuggets** you will need to buy enough shark meat to give as many people as you are serving two small nuggets each, approximately 4 cm (1½ inches) across each way, and 1.5 cm (½ inch) thick. You will also need several limes, curry powder, freshly ground black pepper, salt, flour and vegetable oil. Cut the steaks into the required size for each nugget and squeeze the juice from the limes on to both sides of the steaks. Leave them to marinade for a couple of hours in the refrigerator. These small nuggets have to be fried, so on a plate put enough flour to dust all your steaks. Mix the salt and pepper into the flour. Coat the nuggets lightly in the mixture. Take a heavy frying pan and coat the bottom with the oil. Heat the oil but do not let it smoke since we do not want that particular flavour to influence the final taste of the shark which should be clean. Lay the flavoured nuggets down in the pan and do not move them again for ten minutes, then turn and do the other side. If you move it, it will stick. Leaving it in this way allows it to build up a moderately crisp golden skin, but do not let the oil get too hot. Serve with chunks of lime.

Another good recipe is for **Sautéd Conch** (octopus will do as well). You will need 125 g (¼ lb) of conch meat, very good extra virgin oil – enough to cover the bottom of a heavy frying pan – 2 very finely chopped cloves of garlic, lime juice and salt to taste. If the thin skin or membrane has not been removed, peel it off, then cut the meat in 3 mm (⅛ inch) thick slices against the grain. A good strong light will show you this. Heat the oil and lower one slice in. If the oil sizzles even very slightly, it is ready to proceed. Watch as the pieces tense slightly and turn them immediately. It should be no longer than a minute or so for each side. Absolute care is needed, but it is worth the trouble. Remove the conch pieces, raise the heat a little and add the skin, if you have it, to enrich the flavour, and the garlic, until it is golden brown. Remove the skin and pour the juices over the conch with a squeeze of lime to taste.

The Portuguese also brought their own methods for cooking tuna to the West Indies. If it is well prepared beforehand it can be very good indeed.

For **Barbecued Tuna Steaks** have ready a fresh tuna steak per person. The marinading paste and sauce is enough for four people. Squeeze the juice of half a large lime, 2 tablespoons of red wine vinegar, 2 tablespoons of olive oil, 1 teaspoon of ground black pepper, 3 cm (1 inch) of peeled ginger, 2 cloves of garlic, 4–6 scallions of spring onions, 1 large onion and a bunch of fresh coriander leaves with the stalks cut off and 2 limes to decorate. Blend all the ingredients to a smooth green paste. Use half of the paste to marinade the tuna for twelve hours. Barbecue it over hot coals, allowing fifteen minutes each side. Garnish the steaks with very thinly sliced rounds of lime. As a variation you could mix 150–200 ml (4–6 fl oz) of *fromage frais* with the remaining half of the paste and serve it chilled as a sauce.

When the Madeirans came to the West Indies, they brought with them a simple and exuberant folk religion. Historians all seem to agree that they were particularly devout. The roots of their faith went deep and their frequent *festas*, a blend of religious fervour and celebration, were fundamental to island life. A few years before the people began to leave for the West Indies in 1819, one Madeiran *festa* in particular struck a passing traveller. He wrote: 'A grand festival is holden in honour of the saint; it begins on the fourth and lasts till the fifteenth of August.' During this time they decorated the church with flags of every nation while fifes and drums played all day in the church porch. Such was the bustle and confusion as they gathered from all over the countryside that the traveller thought it was 'not unlike the appearance of an English fair'.

The newly arrived Madeirans in the West Indies – both traditional Catholics and the newly converted who still adhered to many of the religious *festas* – were heavily criticized by those of the Anglo Saxon culture for the simplistic exuberance and expression of their folk religion. Above all, they looked on dubiously as the Madeira wine flowed and spirits rose, lacking any understanding of the overt delight the Portuguese took in celebrating their passion for their church, their God, the mother of God and all their saints. To such onlookers, great drinking meant only saturnalia.

Bishop Etheridge was a Jesuit who left a diary in which he observed the plight of the Portuguese and saw their need to express their faith in celebration as vital. He wrote: 'Portuguese . . . must be and can only be kept in any sort of way to Church and their duties by ceremonies and practice something like what they have been accustomed to in Madeira.' Even the Colonial Office recognized that the spiritual health of the new Portuguese workers depended on the Government seeing to it that more clergymen were brought in from Madeira.

In Guyana, throughout the year in the various parishes, each church celebrated over half a dozen *festas*. The church and its yard were bedecked with flower garlands and flag poles and people arrived on foot from miles around in the surrounding countryside. Fireworks deafened their arrival and competed with military bands which welcomed them. Booths and stalls abounded. The Royal Gazette recorded in 1858 that those Portuguese who were beginning to make their way helped the poor in the community through the *festas*. On the most renowned *festa*, *Nossa Senhora de Monte*, a hearty dinner was given to each needy person along with a plate, bread, a towel and a few shillings. On the day of St Anthony there was a special distribution of bread to the poor. Young people broke eggs into glasses of water to read their futures. Whatever shape the broken egg took would tell their fate: marriage, travel, a star or success.

Much of the meat served on such special occasions came from the wild game that roamed around the estates: manicou, a kind of wild rodent; lapp, which was a type of local rabbit and the quenk, a little wild pig that was always, as Yseult Bridges wrote, 'blundering across their path and into the undergrowth'.

Here again you would find a marriage of African and Portuguese styles of ingredients and preparation. The African had learned to marinade in white rum the strong gamy meats and the Portuguese added his wine to the cooking.

Hare in White Rum and Allspice is a recipe that blends white rum and white wine superbly well. For two people you will need 2 back legs of hare, salt, freshly ground black pepper, 2 large cloves of garlic and 4–6 tablespoons of good white well-perfumed rum such as Jamaican Appleton Special. Remove the membrane from the legs of the hare and score the flesh diagonally across the grain of the muscle in two or three places on each side. Place in a dish and rub the salt, black pepper and crushed garlic all over the meat and well into the cuts, pour over the white rum, cover with cling film to seal in the flavour of the rum and leave to marinade in the refrigerator for twenty-four hours, occasionally turning the meat in the juices. To cook the hare you will need 50 g (2 oz) of unsalted butter, 1 tablespoon of good extra virgin olive oil, 1 small whole chilli, 8–10 freshly ground allspice berries, 4–6 fresh sprigs of West Indian thyme or half a teaspoon of dried thyme, 1 medium onion, 1 tablespoon of finely chopped celery stalk, 1 tablespoon of finely chopped parsley, 2 tablespoons of diced carrots and, finally, 6 tablespoons of dry white wine. Dry the hare legs thoroughly and put the marinade aside. In a heavy pan heat the butter and oil slowly, and put in the chilli tied to a piece of string so that you can retrieve it much later. Great care must be taken to see that it does not burst. Turn up the heat and brown the legs each side, keeping a well-fitting lid on all the time. Add the onion, celery and carrots, chopped as finely as possible, with the coarsely ground allspice, thyme and parsley. Add a little more salt carefully; this will help the meat to sweat its juices. Cover again and when the onions have quite softened in twenty to twenty-five minutes, heat the marinade and white wine to near boiling and add to the pot. Simmer slowly, turning the meat regularly until it is soft. This is quite delicious and very characteristic of the Caribbean way of preparing gamy meats.

The lapp, or rabbit, was then plentiful and easily caught and roasted over an open fire on hot charcoal. For four people marinade a **rabbit** that you have cut up into small pieces in olive oil, 1 crushed clove of garlic, 1 finely chopped Spanish or other mild onion, the juice of a third of a large lime, plenty of freshly ground black pepper, 1 teaspoon of sea salt, 2–3 sprigs of fresh West Indian thyme, 125–150 ml (3–4 fl oz) of white rum and 3 crushed pimento or bay leaves. Keep 50 ml (2 oz) of melted butter for the basting. Rub all the other ingredients carefully into the pieces of rabbit. Score the flesh deeply to the bone to help the flavours penetrate the meat and refrigerate, covered, for twenty-four hours. To roast over an open fire or grill, wipe the flesh quite clean of the marinade. Melt the butter in a bowl and lay the pieces of flesh on a wire grill over the coals; baste with the butter regularly. Allow fifteen minutes for each side.

This meat is delicious if you accompany it with the following salad, which again introduces the liking the Portuguese had for using chorizo, and the African love of ackee which was brought from their own West Africa. When the fruit ripens bright red, it splits open and the creamy, brain-like segments are ready to eat.

For **Chorizo and Ackee Salad** for four people choose a mix of the freshest crispest leaves of watercress, batavia and frissé. You will need to fry 2 finely sliced shallots and 1 sliced clove of garlic in a little olive oil for a few minutes, then add 8 slices of chorizo chopped finely or 8 well-chopped strips of smoked streaky bacon. Fry for another three to four minutes. Add 250 g (8 oz) of tinned ackees (drained from the brine), fresh would be wonderful if available; just simmer them gently for fifteen minutes in a little salted water. Stir in carefully so that they do not break. Add 2 teaspoons of good red wine vinegar, a pinch of freshly ground mace and black pepper. Put in the lettuce and watercress leaves, a squeeze of fresh lime or lemon juice and salt to taste. Turn off the heat and stir gently to coat them in the oil and other ingredients. Cover the pan with a lid for the leaves to warm through for a few seconds. Do not let them go limp.

As the Portuguese and Africans worked so closely, side by side, their Christian and pagan beliefs became intermingled. The African clung to his previous beliefs and folk tales, grafting them onto Christianity, whereas the Portuguese – and other groups – also learned to fear the *soucouyant*, a legendary spirit who survived the crossing from West Africa. Tradition had it that it liked to suck the blood of its victims. At Easter time everyone throughout the island would discuss the coming confrontation between the evil *soucouyant* and the risen Christ. A local newspaper in Grenada ran a marvellous story just after the turn of this century, which shows how very seriously the matter was taken. One Easter, when the demand for bread, cakes and Easter buns was so great that the bakery was working right through the night, the bakery employees, all of African descent, were talking of the *soucouyant*. There was 'grave concern over the stealthy movements of this wicked creature about the town bent on devils work . . . their speculative fever raising by the minute and doubtless fuelled further from the intense heat from the ovens that would be firing all through the night.' As the Catholic church struck twelve, a gust of wind set the door shuddering on its rusty hinges and the thirty men left as one, not to return until Easter was safely over. The townspeople presumably mourned the loss of their Easter baking, but would have been united in sympathetic understanding, for everyone had enough imagination to summon up the imaginary dreaded white sepulchred figure.

There is almost no trace today of the Portuguese cakes and bread, save for rather unappetizing heavy pastries with gaudy yellow and red streaks of articifial colourings. I have, however, come across one local recipe for Portuguese sweet bread, which is very good. Its rich yellow colour is achieved naturally, for the eggs used come from hens that are reared on golden corn meal. The dough behaves very strangely in the making and does need patience, but it is rewarding when you toast it for breakfast with good coffee. It was doubtless made at *fiesta* time and would have been one of several breads they would have given to the poor.

 For **Sweet Bread**, Portuguese style, prepare 30 g (1 oz) of yeast by putting it in a bowl and covering it with 250 ml (8 fl oz) of luke warm water, adding a teaspoon of white sugar. Stir occasionally with a fork to see that it is mixed in well. After about fifteen to twenty minutes it will have frothed up. While this is developing, cream together 50 g (2 oz) of unsalted butter and 125 g (4 oz) of white sugar. Add 2 well-beaten eggs and beat for a few moments to mix in thoroughly. In a large bowl put 375 g (12 oz) of white flour and a teaspoon of salt, make a well in the centre and pour in the creamy mix of eggs, butter and sugar, and the yeast. With a knife carefully turn the mixture over repeatedly to form the dough. Knead on a floured board for about five minutes. Put in an oiled bread tin, cover with a plastic bag and be prepared to wait up to eight hours for it to double in size. Bake in a moderately hot oven for ten minutes and for fifteen to twenty minutes at a moderate heat. The loaf will turn a lovely dark golden colour and is extremely light in texture. Allow the bread to cool in its tin before turning out.

As new generations of Portuguese grew up, they began to travel out from Guyana and Trinidad to settle in other islands such as Grenada. Some even went as far as the east American seaboard. At the same time tradition began to be broken: they adopted the English language, 'although some had picked up the local patois which was more akin to their own Portuguese dialect', and left the Scottish church to build their own Portuguese church. By the 1880s Portuguese and English children were attending school together and adults were marrying outside their own community. Mendes wrote:

> Swarthiness is a frequent characteristic of the Portuguese, not only in the West Indies but in Madeira . . . for two Trinidad-born generations inter-marriage was the rule, after which inter-marriage with other European creoles, blacks and mulattoes and with Chinese began to occur – and today there is little of the hazardous practice of inbreeding left.

When they left the estates and labouring, most moved into menial or more modest jobs in the retail trades in the towns and later began businesses of their own. Strangely, given their seafaring traditions, the Portuguese rarely became fishermen. Perhaps it was the Africans' struggles to make secure their new way of life and income in market gardening and fishing after emancipation, that made the Portuguese hold back from following the same path.

Mendes gives us an account of the business of his grandfather who called himself 'a provisions merchant'. His father's stock-list included 'Madeiran fireworks for the Christmas season and puncheons of Madeiran wine'. They also imported Madeiran onions and saltfish. His grandfather graduated from the retail shop to a wholesale store, which apparently took him into the merchant class. His store was in Almond Walk, now Broadway, in Port of Spain. Almond trees were planted which bore edible fruit that, when ripe, deepened to a reddish purple hue. These lined the green verge and gave shade to the street along which there were similar stores, or rum emporiums, run by other Madeirans. The branches were kept low, trained in parasol fashion, and the broad rounded wax-textured leaves lent shade to the tables which were set out with bottles of the imported Madeiran wines. There was much laughter, drinking and playing of cards and a need to recapture old times.

Fried slices of roasted aubergine (known locally as melongene) marinaded in lime juice, combinations of different and seasonally available seafoods in piquant tomato sauce, small morsels of octopus and the famed garlic pork would all have been delicious. Where the Portuguese landed in the greatest numbers, the locals still take great pride in their garlic pork, a dish which certainly goes back to Madeiran days. Ligon ate it, writing that the meat 'was full of nerves and sinews, strong meat and very well conditioned: boyl'd tender and with Spanish vinegar.' Today the pork meat is parboiled, then dressed with garlic and herbs and steeped for two days in good vinegar.

It is interesting that this dish is regularly made today in Guyana and Trinidad. The recipes of local people all seem to vary slightly, but the final taste is meant to be of a subtle pickled flavour. I choose this recipe because I am interested not only in the use of Spanish vinegar but also the mix of lime and lemon juice.

For **Garlic Pork**, Guyanese style, for six people take a 1 kg (2 lb) piece of pork, preferably from the leg, then crush 500 g (½ lb) of garlic into a paste with a little lukewarm water. Score the meat deeply and rub it in with some thyme, salt and the juice from 1 lime and 1 lemon, then rub in 60 g (2 oz) of Spanish vinegar or acetic acid. Marinade this for at least twenty-four hours or as long again – the longer the better. When you are ready to cook it, wipe off all the marinade and seasonings and cut into small 1·5 cm (½ inch) cubes. Fry in deep oil and serve with cold hard-boiled eggs; these are a bland counterpart to some of the pickled flavour.

For the **Limed Melongene** you will need to have a good heavy olive oil, salt to taste, and some freshly squeezed lime juice. Slice the melongene lengthways in 6 mm (¼ inch) thick slices and salt each side and squeeze the lime all over them. Leave for one hour, then without washing off the resultant juices, fry in shallow olive oil for a few minutes each side, or until the flesh is slightly crisp and golden.

A very refreshing dish to eat while drinking in the heat of the day is the following **Caribbean Seafood Cocktail**. This is served in a chilled glass and the seafood is in a delicious and unusual sauce. You will need to have prepared 125 g (¼ lb) each – or any other combination which suits the seafood available – of peeled prawns, cooked mussels, oysters, or octopus. The octopus needs to be chopped into small pieces and boiled plain in water for an hour and a half until tender. Take a large bowl and put in salt and black pepper to taste, a few drops of pepper sauce, half a teaspoon of wine vinegar, a quarter of a very finely diced onion, the juice of 1 lime, 1 medium gherkin, 1 tablespoon of capers, 2 tablespoons of chopped fresh coriander leaves and 500 ml (16 fl oz) of good tomato juice. Add the seafood and chill for an hour before serving. It is important that when you make this for the first time you taste the juice, for you may like to adjust the amounts of salt, lime juice and wine.

Emigration from Madeira continued at a slower rate until the 1870s and was finally ended in 1882. Many of the Portuguese had gone to the Essequibo river to mine gold, while others went to America. For those who remained in Guyana, some rose to notable positions, owning a good deal of the property outside the sugar plantations. While numbers of new wealthy Portuguese returned to Madeira to see their ancestral home, it became the custom to send their children to school in England and English became their main language.

With financial security it became possible for families to take holidays and observe life in the other islands. The Trinidad branch of the Mendes family went to meet their cousins in the neighbouring island of Grenada, who had prospered by building up a very successful bakery. Mendes wrote: 'Every morning the whole tribe of us would walk to the Fontenoy beach and on our return would stop to buy salt fish dip and bakes.' The ingredients in the dip are very similar to *brandada* found in the Mediterranean.

 For the **Saltfish Dip** for four people you will need to prepare 175–250 g (6–8 oz) of good quality salt-cod. Soak it for twenty-four hours, skin and pull the flakes apart. Take each flake and draw the blade of a sharp knife, pressing down and away from you, across the grain of the flesh. This will break the flakes down into tiny fibrous shreds very easily. At this stage check for bones and remove them. Taste to see if the fish is too salty; if so, pour cold water over it, sloosh the fish around in it, then drain through a sieve, pressing down hard to remove all the water. Remember, however, that quite a bit of salt is needed in the saltfish to come through the addition of cream and eggs. Fry a finely sliced medium onion in 25 g (1 oz) of unsalted butter and 1–2 tablespoons of olive oil until quite soft and season with pepper; add the saltfish and stir together well. Add 125–150 ml (5 fl oz) each of thick and single cream, and the very well-beaten yolks of three eggs. This must all be heated very slowly. On no account must the mixture boil. Serve this with the hot bakes, which are a traditional way of cooking a basic kind of bread roll very quickly, since they are only made of flour and water with a little baking powder added. Today the baking powder can be substituted

with ready-to-use yeast that does make them lighter. Despite the convenience of this yeast, many people still prefer the old method and stick to it. The following recipe is my variation.

To make a dozen **Hot Bakes** put 15 g (½ oz) of yeast in a bowl and cover it with 120 ml (4 fl oz) of lukewarm water, adding ½ a teaspoon of white sugar. Stir occasionally with a fork to see that it is mixing in. After about fifteen to twenty minutes it will have frothed up. While the yeast is working cream together 25 g (1 oz) of unsalted butter and 75 g (2 oz) of white sugar. Add a well-beaten egg and stir into the creamed butter and sugar to mix thoroughly. In a large bowl put 150–175 g (6 oz) of white flour and half a teaspoon of salt; make a well in the centre and pour in the creamy mix of egg, butter and sugar. With a knife carefully mix the ingredients together to form the dough. Knead on a floured board for about five minutes, then leave for an hour or so. While the dough will be springy, you will not notice any great rising. Pull off small pieces, roll them into small balls in the palm of your hand, and gently flatten to approximately 2 cm (¾ inch) in depth. You can shallow fry these in corn or coconut oil. Drop them into fairly hot but not smoking oil and cook on each side for five to seven minutes. They will puff up and turn a beautiful golden colour. The slight sweetness contrasts well with the saltfish.

As much as the descendants of the once indentured Portuguese were establishing themselves as part of the new island way of life, they stood awkwardly between two worlds, for they were still not considered white. The Governor of Trinidad wrote back to England: 'Society in Trinidad is divided into castes as strongly marked as those of Hindustan.' One telling account of the Portuguese social position was given by an English woman. 'Mina was the daughter of a wealthy Portuguese, and she arrived at school each morning in a smart carriage, heavily adorned with jewellery and wearing a silk frock. She was darkly pretty and had long black curls.' Darkly pretty was an innocent enough allusion, but a revealing one. The writer took the trouble to inform her readers that the school was no longer attended only by English girls; 'indeed any whose parents could afford the fees' were now allowed there. By contrast, Mendes wrote:

Never had there been heard in our own parents home one single word or sentence savouring of racial prejudice . . . I don't think this was deliberate on their part: it just never occurred to them that a difference between a fair skin and a dark skin was of any consequence. Would that parents all over the island possessed the kind of sagacity and plain decency.

MANDARINS AND RICE GROWERS

Mountain water that fell white from the mill wheel
sprinkling like petals from the star apple trees
and all the windmills and sugar mills moved by the mule
on the treadmill of Monday to Monday.

Derek Walcott

The Jamaican landscape that was so familiar to planter and labourer alike in the eighteenth century began to change quite dramatically in the nineteenth century. Sugar continued to be the mainstay of the economy, but under the stress of rising costs and falling sugar prices, the planters began to move the cane fields lower down the mountain slopes to the innumerable valleys, coastal areas and river deltas, which were often swampy and fever-ridden.

However, the mountain sides did not return to the wild. The freed Africans began purchasing a few acres of the abandoned sugar estates, while others turned the less accessible areas of virgin estate lands higher up the slopes into quite profitable market gardens. As they did so, the coffee cultivators were also moving in, planting and quickly eroding one mountain side after another.

Coffee growing had begun in the Blue Mountains in a small way a hundred years earlier, after Louis IV had received coffee plants, thought to have originated in the Yemen of which one survived the journey in 1720 to Martinique and, from there, it was taken to Jamaica, becoming renowned worldwide as the 'blue mountain' variety. The climate was found to be perfect for the red and green coffee beans, which show clearly when they are ready to be harvested. Here the sun rises late and the mists swirl high above in the more inaccessible crevices of the Blue Mountains, the mossy floors of the valleys are a verdant green, and the skies – immeasurably high – are periwinkle-blue and peaceful. The most valued beans are called locally the 'rat bite', since, if they can, the rats chew the juiciest beans off the bushes. Once collected, the beans are immediately fermented and ground.

With the success of the coffee production, the continuing strength of the sugar market and the loss of the Africans as a work force, labour remained a problem. The Portuguese had shown their dislike of estate life, and as soon as their contracts expired they left. Yet again, another solution had to be found. The importation of Chinese labour had first been proposed to the British Government by the Governor of Trinidad as early as 1802, on the grounds that two Chinese labourers with a light plough and buffalo brought from home would do the work of forty slaves. The case was still being considered some forty years later by Lord Stanley, Secretary of State, who thought that the Chinese were the most desirable of all the possible pools of labour, because they were intelligent, willing to work for wages and 'would bring their frugal and industrious habits, as well as being able to support the labour of sugar cultivation'.

There had been a precedent – Chinese labour had been used in Cuba from the beginning of the nineteenth century. However, the Chinese Government were not disposed towards it continuing after reports of brutal treatment on the plantations and the high seas trickled back home. But there was nothing they could do to stop those who wanted to leave, seduced away from overcrowded villages, periodic drought and great floods, which destroyed their crops and animals, endangered their own lives and brought them to the point where one more poor harvest would mean famine. Besides this the Taiping Rebellion, one of the bloodiest civil wars in history, had laid waste large stretches of land. As a local saying from the southern provinces of Fukien and Kwangtung put it, 'To be free from floods for three successive years would be to adorn our hogs with shining rings of gold.' It was in this area and, in particular, from two ethno-linguistic groups, the Puriri and Hakka, that the recruiting agents found most of those who were willing to be taken to the other side of the world. They were also reputed to be people from a poor background or social outcasts because of their addiction to opium.

The first two boatloads arrived under sail in 1854, after a voyage that took three months. Perhaps after the rough seas and relatively high mortality and illness, the recruits wondered at their earlier eagerness to leave China. A few were brought to the smaller islands, such as Grenada, but the majority were taken to Jamaica, Trinidad and Guyana. Sugar development had scarcely started in the last two islands when slavery ended, but now labour was desperately needed.

One wonders what the Chinese felt about their new situation in the Caribbean, working under the dazzling sun in the cane fields. The loneliness of their new lives was probably greater than that of any other group who made the transition either before or after: they were relatively few in number and isolated by their different language. A descendant of one of the families who made the crossing told me that the first generation of Chinese settlers spoke over two hundred different dialects, which often locked them within their own family group. Since all the groups were kept busy simply surviving, no one took the trouble to communicate. They bore an added humiliation in that the English did not take the trouble to write their names correctly, but gave only an approximation or the name of the estate or its owner. Even today you will find very often that a Chinese person will carry the name of the estate or its owner plus only a close approximation of his own family name.

Most of all, though, those long lines of men working away in the fields in their traditional loose jackets and blue cotton trousers, suffered from a lack of female companionship. In Guyana, for example, it was estimated that the ratio was four women to every hundred men. The recruiting agencies saw little profit in indenturing women whose feet had been crippled by binding them. In any case, they were happy to be excused from having to consider females, since it was obviously much more profitable to use males on the plantations.

Also the pattern of Chinese life and duties of ancestral veneration traditionally fell upon the women, making it difficult for them to escape the ancestral village. They had to visit the tombs of recently departed kinsmen at least twice a year to care for the souls and provide them with food and money, then perform the rites of lighting the feast incense and offering a roast pig. Traditions were considered very important and, no matter how poor the family was, a great effort was made to celebrate them as well as possible.

One of the most important festivals, called 'double ten' in Trinidad today – that is, the tenth day of the tenth month of the year – is a national holiday. Whatever can be afforded, from southern Chinese-style red meats to duck and shrimp, which until recently were cheap and bountiful in Trinidad, is prepared and cooked.

 For **Roast Pork** for eight to ten people choose a leg with as little fat on it as possible, and weighing about 5 kg (10–11 lbs). Rub the skin with salt and limes, then rinse and score the skin. Now make a marinade of 100–125 g (4 oz) of brown sugar, 2–3 tablespoons of light soya sauce, 8 cloves of garlic, 100–125 g (4 oz) of freshly peeled ginger, black pepper and 3–4 tablespoons of dark rum. Blend this to a paste and rub into the meat. Seal the meat very carefully in heavy foil and put in the refrigerator overnight. Cook in a hot pre-heated oven for thirty minutes, then for another two and a half hours at a low temperature. Remove the foil and return to a high heat for another thirty minutes to let the skin crisp, but not crackle. At this stage you must watch carefully, for the juices will run into the pan. As they begin to thicken and caramelize, baste the joint. To serve, remove the pork on to a serving board and thicken the remaining juices with the arrowroot or corn flour.

The Chinese lived up to Lord Stanley's expectation that they would be excellent workers, and were described as the best plantation workers 'for expertness and really natty work'. This was hardly surprising given the strength and sophistication of agricultural practices in China. Both technically and scientifically, China was far in advance of Europe; heavy mould-board ploughs were in common use and they even had mechanical seed distributors. The peasants completely devoted their lives to intensive farming and usually left home to live in temporary huts in the fields from the first sowing to the harvest. The tools given to them to use in the West Indies were not what they were accustomed to in China, and this was the cause of much dissatisfaction.

They were put to work in the fields to dig drains, drill stumps and trenches, supplied only with hoes, shovels and forks. For all this, and despite the fact that it was often commented upon that the Chinese rose early and laboured hard, they were as exploited and abused as the groups brought in before them. The planters were bound by contract to feed, house and provide the Chinese with medical care, but the reality was very different. Upon arrival at the plantations, they were put in very rudimentary quarters in the barrack building in the old 'negro yard'.

Where the plantations were situated on small islands in the unhealthy low-lying mouth of the Essequibo river in Guyana, the mortality rate was high in the early years. All day long the men had to face the tall cane grass which towered over them, threatening as a grey-green sea surge, and secreting in its cool grass chambers myriad hazards: scorpions, snakes, lice and razor-edged leaves, which easily sliced flesh.

At first, at least, we know that the men cooked for themselves. Their kitchens were overcrowded, with poor ventilation, sanitation and water supplies, and very dubious cooking facilities. Well into this century, Chinese kitchens in the Caribbean remained improvized affairs, often equipped only with a wok, cleaver, spatula and the dearly loved cutting board made of wood that matured through the years.

Rations were limited, and at the best of times nothing like the variety to which even the poorest Chinese would have been accustomed was available. Few of the necessary spices and flavourings that could have been transported would have survived the length of journey or the heat. Soya sauce, dried noodles and five-star powder were available by the end of the century, but sweet and sour plums, fermented black beans and many other such ingredients only made their appearance very recently. In the early years it is even unsure whether rice would have been available. A hundred years earlier there are accounts of it being served to some of the Africans, but this seems to have been variable, for when it ran out they were given mackerel instead. This lack of basic ingredients seems to have been the main reason why the number and type of traditional Caribbean-Chinese recipes seem to have remained so restricted.

Noodles supplied the staple carbohydrate. A restaurateur in Grenada described to me her childhood memories of her father preparing the noodles for the family in the time-honoured way his father had done and his father before him. Sitting in the centre of the kitchen, working at the wooden board or table of 10 cm thick bamboo, he would sometimes knead as much as 4–10 kg of dough, spreading it across the board floured with arrowroot, then lifting and folding it over and over again, always putting more arrowroot flour in between the layers to keep them separate. As he cut them into wafer-thin strips with one end of a bamboo pole strapped down to the wooden board, he would hang them on poles from the ceiling to dry.

Mrs Chung-Steele, of the Bird's Nest Restaurant in Grenada, talked to me at length of the tradition her family sought to maintain in the West Indies. The stock-pot was an important part of kitchen life. Fresh chicken and beef bones were thrown in (pork was used too, but not so often, since many did not like it) and covered with cold water. This was brought to the boil and simmered gently until lunchtime. No herbs were used in it. Spices such as five-star were difficult to get and, to begin with at least, they would not always have been available. Throughout the morning the pot would be carefully skimmed to remove any fat, and for the rest of the day it was dipped into, either to drink as it was, or to be used as a basis for other dishes as they could afford them. The most popular and well-known Chinese dish in the Caribbean today is chow mein. Its success probably lies in the fact that the basic ingredients, such as the stock and noodles, were usually available in the home. Now freshly made noodles are beginning to be a more regular feature in the larger food stores.

To make **Chow Mein** for two people I use a local chicken weighing 1–1.5 kg (2–3 lbs), taking the meat off the bone after roasting and using the carcass to make the stock. Rub salt and white pepper into the bird, cut off the legs and roast in an open pan in the oven for fifty minutes. Free-range West Indian chickens produce a beautiful jelly. Pick off and shred the meat. Put the carcass and giblets into a pot with some onions, cover with 600 ml (1 pint) of water and add 1 chopped medium onion, 3 cloves of garlic and a little white pepper. Bring to the boil and simmer for thirty minutes. You only need 4 tablespoons of stock for the recipe. Refrigerate the rest for later use. Meanwhile, prepare the other ingredients: 3 cm (1 inch) of fresh ginger peeled and sliced along its length into slivers, 1 chopped clove of garlic, 2 scallions or spring onions (chop the white section into 3 cm (1 inch) lengths and the green part very finely), 250 g (8 oz) cooked noodles and 100–125 g (4 oz) of grated pumpkin. Also have ready vegetable oil for frying, 2 tablespoons of light soya sauce, half a teaspoon of dark brown sugar and 1 tablespoon of dry sherry. Fry the garlic, ginger and the white part of the scallion in a heavy pan in some vegetable oil for two to three minutes, then add the shredded chicken for another two minutes, stirring well. Put in all the remaining ingredients, adding 4 tablespoons of the chicken stock to moisten, and finish cooking over a high heat for three to four minutes.

Another noodle-based dish which seems to produce expressions of fond memories is pow, small dumplings with a pork filling. Why it evokes nostalgia I am not sure, for the preparation is lengthy. Perhaps it represents times gone by, when the Chinese depended on each other very much for survival and the community was much closer-knit.

I was told in detail how to make pow, but have not done so for it is apparently a labour of love. Instead I have turned to Rita Springer, the author of *Caribbean Cookbook*, for precise instructions. The filling today is usually diced roast pork, a luxury that would have been beyond many Chinese. Until recently they simply used pork fat, seasoned as the meat filling is today.

 For **Pow** for three to four people you need 1 cup of diced roast pork, 1 teaspoon of soya sauce, half a teaspoon of salt, 1 teaspoon of sugar, 1 teaspoon of Ve Tsin or MSG (optional), 1 tablespoon of cornflour, 120 ml (4 fl oz) of water and 2 tablespoons of cooking oil. The pork is fried in the oil for a few moments, then the soya and seasonings added along with the cornflour, which is blended with water before being added to the pan. Cook for another few minutes. The dough is made with 375 g (12 oz) of flour, 1 tablespoon of sugar, 1 teaspoon of baking powder, half a teaspoon of salt, 60 ml (2 fl oz) of hot water and 2 tablespoons of peanut or corn oil. Sift the flour (until recently this was necessary for the standard 'counter flour' which was rough). Add the baking powder and salt. Dissolve the sugar in hot water. Let this cool. Make a well in the centre of the flour, pour in the sugar-water and add the oil. Mix together and knead a little. Make into a ball which you then flatten into 8 cm (3 inch) rounds. Put a teaspoon of the filling of your choice in the middle and draw the edges towards the centre. Pinch the dough to close and there you have your dumpling. Steam for twenty minutes and eat while hot. This recipe makes approximately a dozen dumplings.

Unlike the Portuguese and Africans, or even the Scottish settlers, the Chinese were very slow to adapt their taste in food and women, or their new way of life. They almost never made use of the varying foods of other groups. Apparently they loathed coconut milk, which was such a general favourite, hated the awful-looking yellow cooking butter which came in traders tins, and insisted on using spices which had come from China. No wonder, then, that it was a common saying that the Chinaman ate no food other than his own – although I should add that I have found they did accustom themselves to the idea of rum as a good marinade for tenderized pork and seafood.

From necessity they also followed the African's traditional way with the coal pot, as did every group before and after. For to light a coal pot and cook everything on the top of it, either directly or in a wok or other pot, would have been the simplest and most convenient thing to do. They cleverly adapted its use to their own food and dishes. They would scale, wash and dry fish – they especially like angelfish – then score the flesh deeply, rubbing salt in and hanging it in the sun for weeks to dry. There was no need to worry about fish that had to be kept fresh, for there was always some available. All they had to do was to light the coal pot, bring a pot of water to the boil and steam the fish over it. They then dipped the fish into a dish that had a mixture of peanut oil with a little garlic and ginger chopped into it. They also treated chicken in the same way.

Another very simple and quick way of preparing fish was to fry it in a pan on top of the coal pot. A modern version of this is made with marinaded tuna.

For **Marinaded Tuna** take slices of tuna cut when still half frozen into 3 cm (1 inch) square pieces. Allow enough tuna for two people and marinade it in light soya sauce and a little cider vinegar, which reduces the 'freshness' of the tuna meat. Refrigerate for two to three hours. In your pan heat a few tablespoons of vegetable oil, but do not let the oil get so hot that it smokes, then dust the tuna slices very lightly in a little flour. The secret is to lay one end of each slice down first, very slowly, and do not attempt to move it. Leave it there for one minute and then turn, and do the other side for exactly a minute. This ensures it will not stick. Serve with wedges of lime.

Simple and quick preparations such as these would have been ideal, for the days in the fields were long, especially during the sugar harvest or 'crop'. The progress of the harvesting was defined by the long lines of heads, bent low and moving in slow uniform rhythm. With two swift, successive, brilliantly curved strokes of the machete, blinding the onlooker as it crossed the sun, the 2 m cane stems were felled. Mule-drawn carts collected the cane, their wheels creaking as they travelled in single file along the badly rutted tracks between the fields. Once the cane was shot under the massive rollers to be crushed for their juice, the air of the countryside by day and by night would be pervaded by the sweet scent of rum.

As the Chinese tried to settle into their new way of life, they began to improve their lot very gradually. Some were allowed to supplement their meagre rations by planting crops in the gardens near their dwellings and in the provision plots at the back of the plantations, as the Africans had done before them. By now there was such a variety of vegetables to be had that they would have been able to make their pickles. Of all Chinese–Caribbean foods, this is probably the one most enjoyed by all groups today. You may use any vegetables or combination of vegetables that you prefer, but I found that the following worked well in the heat and were refreshing.

To make **Pickled Mixed Vegetables** peel and slice 750 g (12 oz) of cucumber, 250 g (8 oz) of carrots, 50 g (2 oz) of salt, 2 tomatoes chopped in quarters, 5–6 florets of cauliflower, 250 ml (8 fl oz) of cider or apple vinegar, 75 g (3 oz) of sugar, half a teaspoon of pickling spices, 3 peeled and very thin slices of fresh ginger. Arrange the vegetables in a deep bowl, sprinkle with the salt and enough cold water to cover. Refrigerate for twenty–four hours. The next day rinse well under running cold water and put all the other vegetables except the cucumber in a saucepan, adding all the other ingredients. Bring to the boil and simmer for ten to fifteen minutes. Add the cucumber and cook for another three minutes. Allow to cool and put in a clean bottle and cover with the mixture. It is said to improve after a week or so; I often make things like this when we first arrive in the tropics since the heat makes you demand something salted or pickled, and so it has never lasted more than a day or so.

By 1870, on ninety-five or so plantations, roughly half of the 5,000 Chinese employed had managed to achieve their own garden plots. Here they cultivated intensively and got reasonable monetary returns. Increasingly they could now be seen joining the succession of vendors calling at the kitchen doors of the great houses throughout the parish at first light, calling in broken speech, 'Pima pepper, cucumbo-o-o, Okola-o-o [okra], Tomato-o-o.'

Here at the kitchen door on the back verandah, the African still ruled, with enormous warmth of heart, concern and affection for all-comers. Before it was even light, the chopping of wood to light the braziers could be heard from the path running up to the back door.

These were used to heat the coffee which had been filtering all night long. Inside the pantry stood the large safe made of wire gauze, inside which the provisions for each day were kept. Its feet always stood in tins of kerosene to prevent the ants climbing up – a trick still used to this day where there are no fridges. Beside the safe stood the large sacks of coffee beans. A panful was given to the cook each morning to be 'patched' as they say. The fragrance as the beans were first patched, then ground, filled every corner of the compound. Then the jugs of the steaming liquid would disappear into the cool recesses of the house, and the tinkle of brass rings could be heard as the mosquito nets were drawn back around the beds.

As the dawn rose, the frail blue light from the flowers on the plumbage hedge merged delicately into the gauze-like mists. Dew still silvered the lawn and the spiders' webs, with their finely spun tracery of threads, glittered in the sun. By seven the cooks from the nearby houses could be seen wending their way along the roads in single file, African-style, to the market, and the *marchands* would start arriving on the verandah, heralding their approach with different calls. 'Turtle eggs! Turtle eggs!' the Africans would cry, holding their delicate wares collected from the sandbanks of the Orinoco river. The eggs had been very lightly boiled and a small hole pricked into each of the fine shells so that grains of salt and pepper could be eased in. Then the whole was placed to the lips and squeezed down the throat.

Throughout the morning the *marchands* would continue to come with trays of produce carried on their heads. They would also bring fowls and ducks and calabashes filled with eggs. The lady of the house would appear occasionally to check the quality. The *marchand* would lavish the produce with praise: 'Yes, Madam, dese t'ree be good.' For fowl, he would produce a hanging scale. The hapless birds were then hung on the hook by the string that bound their feet. If bought, they were then sent off amid much squawking protestation to have their wings cut, and to enjoy a short freedom in the run before being sent to the pot.

The Chinese *marchands* had several specialities apart from the vegetables they grew. One was watercress gathered from the fast-moving water under the sugar mills. In many cases the planters had been reluctant to introduce mechanical advantages to the estates, but by the time the Chinese arrived there were some improvements in agricultural equipment, such as steam engines and vacuum pans. Today, in the country areas, one may still come across the enormous iron wheels forged during the Industrial Revolution and brought from England. They are usually half buried beneath the crumbling stone walls of the old boiling houses, and under the viaducts that carried the water down from high in the mountains to turn the wheel. The perpetual grinding of lives and hopes lies buried and forgotten in the grasp of gnarled old roots, lichens and epiphytes.

Today, where the old viaducts have not collapsed, the water still flows in a steady stream, and here you will find copious supplies of watercress. The conditions are ideal, for the beds are fed by water that bubbles along constantly at a perfect temperature, shaded by the stone of the ancient viaduct. Watercress needs a steady flow of sparkling clear water of at least 11°C. Take a knife and cut the leaves off with 5–7 cm of the stem. The gap left will be replenished next day, so fast is the growth. The leaves are dark green, bright and larger than I have ever seen in Europe, with a peppery bite to them all through the year.

The Chinese recognized how good the cress was, and according to the diarist, Yseult Bridges, cut it in the very early morning, carrying it along in two baskets slung from each end of a bamboo pole that they bore on their back across the shoulders. I imagine them jogging along country traces through a landscape unimaginably different from that at home in China, in the early morning, with the mists dripping and freshening the new golden blooms of the cat's claw vine. These would blossom with a suddenness that is breathtaking in its beauty, their perfumed nectar seducing hosts of insects, bees and birds such as thrushes of an azure blue, golden orioles and humming birds, whose foreheads signal flashes of iridescent green as they hover and draw subsistence.

The Chinese use watercress in their soups, while the Africans, influenced by the English tradition, put a couple of sprigs into their souse, or serve it fresh alongside black pudding and souse. One of the best local soups I have eaten was made with a fish called trigger. Locally it is also called 'old wife' or, in Grenada, *boose*. Its appearance is of incomparable beauty, with a skin of deepening grades of blue, and firm but delicate flesh like a John dory, which would be a good substitute.

For **Fish and Watercress Soup** for two people you will need a bunch of watercress with the stalks removed, then marinade 500 g (1 lb) of fish in 1 tablespoon of cider vinegar, a dash of pepper sauce, salt and a quarter of a teaspoon of peeled and freshly grated ginger. Rub gently on to the skin and inside, and leave for two hours. Heat gently 250 ml (8 fl oz) each of freshly made chicken and fish stocks. The fish stock is easily made by gently simmering the heads of your fish in enough water to cover for ten minutes. Add approximately 1½ tablespoons of light soya sauce, 1 tablespoon of cider vinegar, 2 tablespoons of dry sherry, some freshly ground black pepper and a pinch of Ve Tsin or MSG powder. While this is heating together, put the vegetable oil into a heavy pan and pat the fish dry, then dust it very lightly in flour to help prevent it from sticking. Heat the oil until a small piece of stale bread turns golden in forty-five seconds. Lower the fish in slowly from one end and leave to fry for four to six minutes. Do not try to move them around in the pan. Fry on each side until the outside becomes crisp. Drain the fish on kitchen paper to remove any oil and drop into the stock, adding the watercress. Remove from the heat immediately and serve at once. You will need to adjust to your own taste the balance of sherry, soya sauce and salt.

For a time in Trinidad the Chinese held a monopoly on oysters, and became known as the oyster *marchands*, crying out, 'Oy-si-ta, oy-si-ta', in the town streets and on the back verandahs. In Elizabethan times, Raleigh recorded 'that he coasted the land' of Trinidad, seeing oysters growing on trees. Strange as this may sound, they do grow there on the mangrove trees, which flourish in marshy places close to the sea. Upon the roots, oysters of a delicate and delicious flavour cling close together like sea olives in great clusters. In those days the oyster abounded. Being smaller than our northern varieties and considered a potent aphrodisiac, up to three dozen oysters could easily be consumed at a time in the last century. Today they are less plentiful and cheap, but all local people believe in their aphrodisiac qualities. In Jamaica they eat them straight with a dash of vinegar and pepper.

It was suggested to me by a Chinese Caribbean that I cook oysters in the following way, marinading them with rum, ginger and garlic, before deep-frying them in batter. When oysters are not available, lambie or conch is a worthwhile creature from the sea to use, because the marinading helps with any toughness. If you are using conch, cut off the dark, tough tips and slice through the body so that it opens like a book. Look carefully for the grain and cut across it, making small pieces of approximately 3 cm (1 inch) square. Abalone is the closest likeness that I can suggest for those with no lambie. If you are making this with oysters, use the smaller, cheaper Portuguese oysters, which still have a good flavour of the sea.

To make the marinade for **Deep-Fried Oysters** for roughly 450 g (1 lb) of oyster, crush a clove of garlic and a small piece of ginger through the garlic press. Mix in with 4–5 tablespoons of white rum and a pinch of white pepper. Leave to marinade overnight. Drain, pat dry and fry quickly for a minute or so in fairly hot shallow oil. Or fry in egg batter, for which you will need 6 tablespoons of cornflour, 1 teaspoon of salt, 3 tablespoons of water and 2 eggs. Put the cornflour into a bowl and make a well in the centre, putting in the beaten egg yolks and water. Beat carefully to make the batter, then leave for thirty minutes. Now whisk the egg whites to form stiff peaks and fold into the batter. Dip the pieces of oyster into the batter and fry in enough vegetable oil to cover them at 190°C (375°F). To test the temperature, first fry a small piece of stale bread, which should turn golden in forty-five seconds.

The Chinese market gardening and vending was much against the planters' will, since at heart they were terrified that their indentured workforce would develop a way of supplementing their living so successfully that they could leave the estates once their term was served. Those who were not allowed vegetable plots and had to depend on rations which were never sufficient, went hungry. Taking matters into their own hands, they began to form nocturnal gangs and raided the local provision grounds and stockyards of neighbouring villages and estates. Where once the plantation owners had feared the African rebellions, now they had to prepare to defend themselves against gangs of twenty to thirty Chinese, armed with machetes tied to long sticks, who regularly terrorized the neighbourhoods. As before, the planter had to arm and trust his watchmen.

Life on the estate still had to continue, while militia and troops were called during the frequent alarms. The estate owners became used to protecting themselves. Laws were passed to curb the gangs: a convicted offender could be flogged in public, up to thirty-nine lashes – mild punishment compared with earlier times. Nonetheless, when the sun set and no moon rose, and the sea turned to a noiseless blackened glass in the windless heat of the night, how did the planter think and feel, sitting on his sugar fortune, trusting no one, yet having to trust the very ones he had abused through the generations?

Although it was widely acknowledged that the Chinese were good workers, some simply could not adjust to life on the plantations and had their contracts rescinded. Others reindentured after being tempted by bonus money, and then very often disappeared with it. In Jamaica many of these drifted into the towns and became vagrants and were arrested.

Others deserted and many died from overdoses of opium. Many of these problems had arisen, as it was suggested in Jamaican Government reports, because whatever the pressures of population in China, each family had become accustomed to living on its own farm or independent small-scale settlements. Therefore, it was arranged by the island's Government that all the dispersed Chinese, except the unfit who were to be kept at the Kingston almshouses, would be rounded up and put together in settlements where they could be reunited with their families. Here they would be able to communicate in their own language and live according to their customs, keeping their traditional habits of food growing and preparation.

It is interesting that, initially at least, the majority preferred to grow sweet potatoes and yams. The true yam had reached China in the sixteenth century, so they did not in this case need the African to teach them how to prepare it. But they soon became discouraged and dissatisfied: it would seem that they were unable to agree on what sort of crop they would grow for themselves. In some cases the land was prepared for rice growing, because it was thought that it would be more profitable. At home, of course, the Chinese would have been accustomed to its regular production. There were more varieties than we could begin to imagine: pink rice, white rice, yellow rice, mature rice and winter rice, each with its own characteristics and some even with an almost flower-like scent.

But turning the land over to rice production was a horrendously hard task. On an estate in the southern states of America, it was noted that to form the banks for the rice, the slaves moved enough earth to build all the pyramids in Egypt. It was only after the middle of the nineteenth century that rice cultivation thrived, and many parts of the landscape in Guyana and Trinidad changed dramatically. Village No. 72 on the Corentyne coast, for example, became known as Hong Kong.

Today as you land at dusk in Trinidad, the last and southernmost island in the archipelago, you can still clearly see the paddy fields laid out all those years ago. At that height they look for all the world like an English landscape, arranged in neat squares. It is only on the ground that they reveal themselves as rice fields.

In the Caribbean the Chinese had to put up with a much poorer quality and variety of rice than at home. Until as recently as twenty years ago, the quality was very unreliable. Part of the relaxation of daily life was to settle down to pick over the rice, removing unwanted objects such as dirt and small stones. Today the quality is improving, much now being imported.

Fried rice became one of the quickest and easiest meals to prepare, for it was a sensible way of using up boiled rice and left over pieces of cooked meat, if there were any, so that nothing went to waste.

 The Caribbean version of **Fried Rice** uses vegetable or peanut oil, and for flavourings anything to hand from ham to cooked pork meat, or shrimps – dropped in boiling water for a minute or two, then peeled – then perhaps a few chopped scallions, some soya sauce, a pinch of Ve Tsin powder and a little white pepper. The oil is heated for frying the vegetables, the cooked rice is mixed in and the seasoning added. In the old days, apparently, when an egg was a luxury, it would have been fried for a minute or two until set, broken up with a fork and stirred in with the other ingredients.

Honey was another ingredient in Chinese cooking which became increasingly available in the West Indies during the nineteenth century, as estate owners successfully learned how to keep bees. They had learned to import the queens from England, Italy and America, slowly cross-breeding to evolve a strain that could flourish in tropical conditions. Yseult Bridges, a child growing up on an estate in Trinidad, wrote many years later: 'I learnt to work the extractor, cut out the queen-cells and drone cells, smoke and open a hive.' Today one often sees neatly painted white hives dotted about in the shade of a hill or cocoa patch, or beside a trace, shaded by overhanging bamboo, its delicate green leaves whispering evidence of the slightest breath of the wind.

Honey and soya sauce make a delicious blend in much recent Chinese-Caribbean cooking. The balance of these two flavours comes down to individual taste, so you will need to experiment. Here is one such recipe which I think is delicious. Five-spice powder is a mixture of ground black pepper, star-anise, fennel, cinnamon and cloves. Allspice or cloves may be substituted if five-spice powder is unavailable.

 Spareribs of Pork in Honey and Soya Sauce, flavoured with five-spice powder and spring onions with ginger. For four to six people rub 3–4 tablespoons of white rum into 4–6 spareribs of pork and pour over a little vegetable oil. Put in a moderate oven to roast. When the ribs are cooked and becoming crisp, remove them. In a heavy pan put 1 tablespoon of vegetable oil and fry 1 clove of garlic and 2 cm (¾ inch) of peeled, fresh ginger. Crush both of these by putting them through the garlic press, add 1 tablespoon or so of clear honey and 3–4 tablespoons of light soya sauce. Taste and try for balance. Now add 1 tablespoon of five-star powder. Stir together well for a few minutes and add the pork ribs. Cover with a lid and simmer gently for twenty to thirty minutes until cooked.

Roasting, then steaming is another Chinese way of cooking pork that I was shown in Grenada; the meat is roasted almost to the crackling stage, then steamed and flavoured with plums. The skin becomes tender and melting and the meat spongy.

In the early 1870s, the practice of reindenturing began to come to an end. Since the Chinese were not entitled to free or assisted passage home, they were almost bound to stay and settle. A few eventually managed to save enough money to return home, but most could not or did not, and made their lives in the West Indies. In Guyana, lobbying was done in an attempt to get land put aside for them so that they could develop their own occupations. Hopetown, some miles inland on the Demerara river – after which the sugar is named – was one of the first such settlements established by the Chinese who had converted to Christianity, in the low-lying, swamp-ridden land around the river which was good for rice growing. The Chinese had always been housed in some isolation on the plantations, and because of this had little contact with the Creoles in rural towns and villages. The isolation was not improved as they moved on to the new settlements, and they largely lived in a self-enclosed world.

On the new settlements the Chinese worked as hard as elsewhere, establishing a variety of crops of their own choosing, such as potatoes, patchoy, ginger, cassava, plantains and bananas. They would have learned how to take care of these last few on the plantation. Some vegetables were even being called after them: coriander, known as Chinese parsley, and yard-long beans, known as Chinese beans. They also began to rear cattle and pigs, and meat became a regular part of their diet.

More traditional dishes from Fukien and the southern coastal regions, where many of the indentured Chinese originally came from, are also still prepared. Fukien is famous throughout China as the producer of the finest soya sauce and many dishes are prepared with it. I was given the following recipe for snapper by Mrs Chung-Steele, the owner of the Bird's Nest Restaurant in Grenada. It shows how the ingredients needed to produce these dishes have become available in the West Indies today. Snapper, of course, was always there, but the subtle use of black mushrooms would not have been used in this way before. Now it is all flown in. She told me that when preparing fish in this way, she uses more ginger than garlic, but that in a similar paste for meat she reverses this, emphasizing the garlic rather than ginger.

For **Snapper with Black Mushrooms** allow 225 g (½ lb) of snapper per person. Leave the head on and score the flesh in diagonal lines on both sides. Mix together the following ingredients: equal amounts of crushed garlic and fresh ginger, a little white pepper, some salt to taste, 4–6 tablespoons of very light quality soya sauce, 2–3 finely chopped scallions or spring onions and 1 tablespoon of dark or red rum, as she called it. Then mix in a pinch of Ve Tsin powder or MSG to further bring out the taste, with two drops of sesame oil. Put the fish in a dish and dress with the mixture, laying two black mushrooms – that have been prepared by soaking for an hour or so – decoratively along the back of each portion. Marinade for ten to fifteen minutes, then place the fish and juices in a double boiler and steam for five minutes.

The following dish of beef and five-spice powder has its origins in Fukien too. In the West Indies before regular supplies were available directly from China, allspice or cloves were sometimes used as a readily available, though not entirely satisfactory, substitute. Now five-spice powder from China is available. It adds a delicious aromatic blend of cloves, black pepper, ground star-anise, fennel and cinnamon. Note also the use of the local demerara sugar in this version.

To make a dish of **Beef and Five-Spice** for two people, you will need 250 g (8 oz) fillet of beef, 3–4 tablespoons of vegetable oil, 125–150 ml (4 fl oz) water, 1 beef stock cube or 125–150 ml (4 fl oz) fresh beef stock, 2 tablespoons of five-spice powder, 2 teaspoons of soya sauce, 15 mm (½ inch) of fresh ginger, 2–3 teaspoons of brown demerara sugar, 25 ml (1 fl oz) white wine and 2 teaspoons of arrowroot. Slice the beef very thinly against the grain into slices 3 mm (⅛ inch) thick. Fry in the oil for thirty seconds or so on each side; remove from the oil and set aside. Drain off all the oil except a teaspoon and use this to crush the stock cube into a paste. Boil the water and slowly add to the mixture until the stock has been formed. Now add the ginger, crushed through a garlic press, and all the remaining ingredients, except the arrowroot. Bring to the boil and immediately lower the heat. Simmer for four to five minutes to reduce a little. Use some of this stock to mix the arrowroot to a paste, stir it back into the stock carefully and cook for a few minutes longer until it has thickened. Turn off the heat, return the meat to the pan and cover with a lid until it has warmed through. The meat must not be allowed to cook any more or it could toughen and lose that juicy succulence of meat fried for only a few seconds. Serve with plain boiled rice.

Continuing our talk in the restaurant, Mrs Chung-Steele told me that while she would like to use arrowroot as a thickening agent, she uses tapioca instead. The arrowroot is grown in great quantities in the neighbouring island of St Vincent, but she could not rely on the local schooners to ship it packed away from barrels of kerosene or pickled meats which ruin the flavour.

In their new lives, the Chinese met new problems. There were regular incidents of violence between the Creoles and the Chinese, who endured tormenting on the streets, and were dishonoured and humiliated for insisting on keeping their traditional pigtail and style of dress. To avoid trouble, one acting governor advised that Africans and Creoles should not be employed as drivers or overseers of the Chinese workgangs.

The Creoles' resentment of new immigrants had begun with the great increase of labour in the middle of the nineteenth century, which had led to competition for the much needed jobs the plantations could offer. However, a lot of the antagonism sprung from sensing the prejudices that the Chinese held against the 'barbarians'. The Chinese regarded the Creoles as ill-educated and, despite their continuing shortage of women, a relationship with a Creole was very rare. One estate owner wrote: 'They do not marry at all, strange to say; and I think their very peace and comfort is due to the absence of women.'

At first the free Chinese had little chance of accumulating any extra money to develop their own business interests. The Portuguese immigrants who had suffered so miserably on the estates and survived, had taken a firm grip on the retail trade and understandably kept it to themselves. As time went by, though, the Chinese gained enough confidence and experience to move into town and try things for themselves. Although a few Chinese managed to save enough money to return home, most of those in Guyana at least, were not entitled to free or assisted passage. So they made their lives in the West Indies, abandoning the sugar estates. Slowly they broke the Portuguese hold on the retail trade. Small shops began to abound, some even being set up on the estates, and it was remarked that it was the exception in one part of Port of Spain to meet any other than a Chinaman: 'All the little by-streets branching therefrom are alive with Celestials of every grade.' They became pharmacists, barbers, hairdressers, laundry men and butchers, and by the end of the nineteenth century held an impressive number of licences for shops entitled to sell anything from 'spiritous liquors' to provisions, wine and malt to opium and ganja, donkey and mule carts to *batteaux*, punts and schooners.

FROM EAST TO WEST

When sunset, a brass gong,
vibrate through Couva,
is then I see my soul, swiftly unsheathed,
like a white cattle bird growing small,
over the ocean of the evening canes,
and I sit quiet, waiting for it to return,
because, for my spirit, India is too far.

Derek Walcott

The southernmost island of Trinidad differs from the others of the archipelago in that it was once part of the South American mainland. To the north and east, the coasts are swept by the Atlantic, watched over by the sinisterly vigilant eye of the brooding *corbeaux*. To the west, when the sun sinks swiftly towards the mainland, the waters in the narrow Gulf of Paria flush salmon, and the world is streaked blood red. Then, the green of the mountains, where you can still find tracts of rainforest, darkens and the winds freshen and cool the night. Twilight only lasts for a few minutes, then all is quite dark, a signal for the musical life of the insects, who inherit the night, to begin. Let one of those nightly contributors – be it cricket, frog, bullfrog, or mosquito – miss a beat, and the silence is thundering.

It was to Trinidad that the majority of East Indians were brought to fill the gap left by the Chinese from the middle of the nineteenth century. A first batch of nearly 400 had been indentured as early as 1838, arriving in Guyana on the *Whitby* and *Hesperus*, but ill-treatment roused the anti-slavery lobby and they were sent home. Recruitment resumed under government control in 1844 after considerable agitating on the part of the planters, who hoped that increased competition for jobs would depress wages and force the African back on the plantations.

For the Indian it was a journey made across the *kala-pani*, or the black waters. For many it was an act of defiance and could mean social ostracism or caste defilement. Nevertheless, it did not deter them.

Some Indians were taken to Jamaica on board the *Athenium* in 1843. As they landed at Falmouth, the morning journal notes that they were cordially welcomed by their black brethren, who generously offered them oranges, sugar-cane and various descriptions of fruit, as well as bread and cakes. There was sound reasoning behind the Africans' immediate generosity. One Captain Comins wrote that the African appeared to welcome the idea that 'a lot of coolies were coming'. They said, 'Make them come now massa, they will buy our provisions fro' we.'

The newly indentured Indians, the last great pool of cheap labour to be tapped by the planters, brought with them a whole new palette of colours, textures, scents and flavourings to the already vivid scene. Burnt *jeera*, cumin, cardamom and *haldi* aromatized the air. Saffron, *alazarin* and indigo, silks and saris, dazzled the eye in great swathes of movement and colour against the blue of the Caribbean sky. During feast days the estates exploded with the sound of beating tassa drums and the ringing of bells and bangles on wrists and ankles. Names such as Ramprasad, Ramcholan, Choonilal and Shama added to the melodic line. White humped cattle and black water buffalo transformed the landscape wherever they settled. Their grey-black thatched huts clustered together deep in the cane or paddy fields, enfolding their lives and customs in sanctity. Here they worked their lives away unnoticed, the luxurious spring freshness of the crops contrasting with the drab sameness of their lives.

They brought their bullock carts with them to replace the mule and they, 'the coolie', replaced the 'Chinee' in the cane lines. The writer, V. S. Naipaul, a child born into an indentured family, described twentieth-century India as a country of feudal princes and a 'peasantry trained in loyalty'. The British Government was therefore able to recruit labour there with ease. The vast majority came from the northern province of Uttar Pradash, speaking a dialect of Hindi. Others, to a much lesser extent, were recruited either in Calcutta and Bombay in the north of the country, or Madras in the tropical countryside to the south. To these points the Indians travelled from many miles around, from the districts of the United Provinces, the Bihari district, the Hills People's district, the Bombay Presidency and Telugu and Tamil districts.

The numbers of recruits fluctuated very much from year to year, largely following the state of the weather: good weather would mean good harvests and cheaper food, so less would be driven to emigrate. But as the population was steadily increasing, and the family plots of land were subdivided again and again, they were becoming un-economical. Many Indians sought the work.

Others were misled. Recently fragments of an account of the life-story of a Trinidad Indian, who claimed to be a hundred years old, were discovered. His account, intertwined with folk-tales and poetry, tells of how he left the foothills of the Himalayas and travelled down the Gangetic plain to seek work. After working for a time on a tea plantation in Assam, he eventually found his way to the emigration depot in Calcutta, and so on to a ship to Trinidad, the island with the largest population of Indians.

On board ship conditions were too overcrowded for them to continue the observance of who was 'touchable' and who was not. All castes and religions had to share facilities and carry out duties indiscriminately.

Barrack life was the final equalizing force; here the rigid divisions between castes were softened and feudal ties broke down. Every caste, from the warrior *kshatriya* to the lowliest leather worker, found themselves indentured so that the social divisions, which were such an integral part of life in India, became latent or even meaningless. While the Indians were the first group to be allowed to keep their culture, food, language and clothing, the habits of different geographical and religious groups very quickly amalgamated around a shared sense of the importance of ritual.

Naipaul wrote of the Indian in the Caribbean as 'governed and protected by rituals which were like a privacy . . . in the Trinidad countryside they created a simple rural India.' This directed cooking and eating as much as any other area of life. Food in its natural state was accepted as 'clean'. To peel and slice and cook was opening the product to contamination. Earthenware dishes could only be used once, so that food was eaten off banana and almond leaves. Animals that died from natural causes could not be eaten; they had to be properly slaughtered. A Brahmin might purchase his fish from an untouchable, providing the latter was not allowed to clean or gut it.

In India there were many conceptions of the way the world was constructed, one of them being that it was made up of concentric continents which encircled the mystic Mount Meru. Each was divided from the other by one of the seven magical oceans representing the basic needs of humanity. The ocean closest to the Mount was made of salt, the next of very rough brown sugar – it is said that the sugar was brought to India from New Guinea in Neolithic times – the third of wine, and the remaining oceans of *ghee*, milk, curds and fresh water. This tells us a good deal about the symbolism of the essential elements in the Indian diet.

The rations issued to the Indians made little allowance for such subtleties. At first the diet was of a very low quality: heavy carbohydrate laced with the occasional vegetable that was in season. Any supplementary foodstuffs issued by the employers were deducted out of an almost non-existent wage. The most families could afford when they arrived, and indeed for many years after, was flour and water to make *roti* or *chappati*. The very poor ate these unleavened breads simply with an uncooked bird pepper, or with a local West Indian variety of spinach called *baji*, which grew wild. Even *dahl* was special then, and meat was very rare. Coconut water, which was plentiful and free, was drunk a great deal. But it was a long time before most of the Indians could afford rice for everyday dishes.

Chappati probably was and still is the most basic of all Caribbean-Indian foods. It is also very cheap to make since a small amount of flour stretches to feed many people. Naipaul wrote:

My ancestors migrated from the Gangetic plain a hundred years ago . . . I know the beauty of sacrifice, so important to the Aryans. Sacrifice turned the cooking of food into a ritual: the first cooked thing, usually a small round unleavened bread, a miniature, especially made, was always for the fire, the God.

The Indian brought his heavy *tawa* to the islands to make *chappatis*, and insists it can be done no other way, but we have made them in a heavy frying pan. I use the following local Caribbean recipe.

For **Chappatis** you will need 225 g (8 oz) of wholemeal flour, some salt, 50 g (2 oz) unsalted butter, 150 ml (5 fl oz) water and 1 tablespoon of *ghee* or oil. The butter must be rubbed by hand into the flour and salt until it is perfectly mixed in and there are no discernible lumps of fat left. Then pour in the water and mix to a dough. Form it into a ball and knead it for at least ten minutes on a floured surface until you feel the elasticity. Set aside for thirty minutes. Divide the dough into small pieces and roll each out to approximately 20 cm (8 inches) in diameter. Heat a heavy pan over a moderate heat, brush the surface with a little oil or melted *ghee*, and put the *chappati* down. When small bubbles or blisters begin to pop up, press down again with a spatula to flatten them out, then turn. The *chappati* will be cooked in a matter of a few minutes and should turn golden.

There is much more mystique concerned with the making of *roti*, the flat unleavened pastry-like bread that has crossed all group frontiers and is today enjoyed by everyone in the Caribbean. It is very difficult to make a good, soft and flexible one, and it takes a great deal of experience. However, when well done, it is superb.

Roti can be made with various ingredients, depending on what can be afforded. With a curried chickpea filling it becomes a *dahlpourri*. Into the well-worked ball of flour and water is pressed a teaspoon of cooked split-pea paste. Then the dough is pinched over it and the ball rolled out like a *chappati* or pancake. This is the great skill of it, for when the *roti* is laid down on the heated *tawa* to cook, the two sides of the dough will lift slightly off the seasoned paste of split peas, so that there are three delicate light layers which have separated cleanly from each other, but are still a strong casing since the edges are firmly closed together.

If economics allow it, *roti* is wonderful served as a wrap for massala fowl curry. Until very recently chicken 'back and neck' was the usual buy for the majority of people in the Caribbean. Next came the chicken wings, having slightly more meat on them. They do make a very good curry for the *roti*. Remove the feet only after cooking for they add to the tastiness of the dish, but leave in the bones for they are an acceptable and expected part of the whole experience.

For **Massala Fowl Curry** for two people prepare 8 chicken wings by making deep cuts into the flesh. Season with the standard seasoning and leave for a few hours. Shake off as much of the seasoning and resulting juices as you can, and pat dry. Using the caramelizing method (see Cook's Notes) fry them in oil and sugar until golden brown, then add 1 large finely chopped onion, a teaspoon of black fresh pepper, salt to taste and 1½ tablespoons of massala or curry powder. Cover with a lid and simmer very slowly until it has sweated out its juices, then add 2 tablespoons of tomato sauce and 1 large well-chopped tomato. Stir in well, then add approximately 250–300 ml (8–10 fl oz) of boiling water. The point is that this curry is to go into the *roti* and must be fairly dry or it will drip everywhere. The sauce should be the consistency of very thick cream. If it is too thin, then reduce vigorously. Do not worry if the meat falls off the bone – the end result is even better.

Wholemeal flour, rough counter flour and the more refined plain flour served all sorts of other purposes to make cheap food which filled many stomachs. *Metai* was flour mixed with sugar, baking powder and water, then fried. If split peas could be afforded, to make a change they were substituted for the flour, soaked overnight, then ground and seasoned with some garlic and onion, and made into little balls called *phulouri* for deep-frying. *Bara* was a salt-cake, this time a mix of flour and split peas, some baking soda and curry powder for seasoning, rolled into balls and deep-fried. Take two of these and put some curried *channa* (chickpeas) between them and you have 'doubles', one of the most popular Caribbean snacks. Failing the financial resources to afford the chickpea filling, a dash of tamarind or mango sauce might be added for flavouring. Today these traditional foods, born of poverty and skilful seasoning, are loved, and the stores even sell ready-to-make mixes of *phulouri* and *accra*.

Accra and floats, another indigenous cheap dish, was a marriage between what was by now a traditional use of salted fish amongst the other groups (except the Chinese) and the Indians' economic dependence on flour.

Recently the Bajan food writer, Rita Springer, recorded her version of **Accra and Floats**. You need to soak 100–125 g (4 oz) of saltfish in water for as many hours as is necessary. Then remove the skin and bones. Mince with the following seasonings: a tablespoon of chopped onion, 1 clove of garlic, 2 blades of shallots or spring onions, a sprig of thyme and a small piece of de-seeded red pepper. In a bowl put 225 g (8 oz) of flour, ½ teaspoon of salt and 7 g (¼ oz) of dried yeast dissolved in a little warm water. Now add 350 ml (12 fl oz) of tepid water, mix this altogether to make a batter and add the fish mixture. It should then be left to stand for two hours. To cook this you will need a deep pan of hot oil. Into this drop the mixture by the spoonful and fry until cooked. More flour is needed for the accompanying 'floats', which are made with 225 g (8 oz) of flour, ¾ teaspoon of salt, 60 g (2 oz) of shortening and 7 g (¼ oz) of dried yeast dissolved in a little warm water. Put together in a bowl and mix with some warm water to make a dough, knead for ten minutes and fry in small balls in hot oil.

If the family were rich enough to own a cow and it had given birth, then the diet was further enriched from the extra milk it was producing. From this they would make *lassi*, an enriching drink made from yoghurt. Otherwise the peasants drank a mixture of brown sugar dissolved into water, with *tulssi* leaves shredded on the top; only later could they have begun to afford expensive sweetened condensed milk. The other important benefit of owning a cow was that it provided milk to make *ghee* from unclarified butter. From a religious point of view, any product cooked in *ghee* was purified. Now it is usually bought in tins, but it was traditional to make it at home. The butter would be carefully melted in a saucepan, great care being taken to see that it never showed a hint of browning. It was heated to just below boiling point and then simmered for roughly thirty minutes, until the moisture in the butter had quite evaporated and the protein sunk to the bottom, leaving the clear fat on the top. It was then strained through several layers of cheesecloth into a storage jar. As it cooled, it would solidify and could then be kept for months in a cool place.

As the years passed, conditions improved. Rice became an extremely important staple food in the Indian diet. It was also the Indian who made the greatest contribution to the rice industry in Trinidad and Guyana. He had grown rice in the Gangetic delta since 2000 BC, and his traditional skills in irrigation brought from India contributed greatly to the success of cultivation in the islands. At first they were adopted by the planter for rice growing, then used on the sugar estates. By 1903 the rice-growing industry had grown significantly. In Guyana alone they were cultivating nearly 1,000 hectares of rice.

The West Indian planter was determined not to help previously emancipated slaves and indentured folk alike to become a peasantry. But times and politics were beginning to change: the notion of greater self-sufficiency and more local food production was beginning to enter the British consciousness. Towards the end of the nineteenth century, the British Government sent the author, Charles Kingsley, to appraise the situation for them in the West Indies. He returned to England with the firm belief that the English should take warning from their own manufacturing system that 'condemns a human intellect to waste itself', and was sure that the West Indian labourer, 'will learn more if he is allowed to till his own provision ground properly than the cane piece.' He added by way of persuasion that it was so in England: 'Our best agricultural day labourers are those who cultivate some scrap of land and prevents their depending entirely on wage labour.' His suggestions for preserving fruits and making plantain meal for the English working classes were never followed, and things remained much the same, with basic supplies and provisions.

Corn meal, flour, salted meats, fish and lamp oil, candles and so on were still being imported across the Atlantic at great expense. Finally, to reduce the expense of bringing the Indians from half-way round the world, the planters were obliged to grant them parcels of land at a nominal rent, which helped the Indian in some cases to leave behind him his squalid existence in the *lodgie*. The contractor would clear this land and plant it with cocoa seedlings shaded with a banana or plantain stool – a group of suckers planted close together – between which he grew his own crops of maize, pigeon peas, aubergines and a range of other vegetables. All that was yielded would be his, but at the end of five years, he received only a small payment for the cocoa trees that had survived before the contract ceased. This system, the first ever in which the planters granted parcels of land for cultivation, was highly advantageous to them. Their land was cleared, which in the tropics meant an enormous effort, and returned to them planted with new trees, while at the same time it yielded rent.

As farmers, the Indians were considered the most successful of all the indentured people to be taken to the West Indies. They could be seen working their new landscape in the time-honoured way, well into this century. Men and women each brought their appointed duties: husbands tended the crops of maize and yam, mounding the earth around them, while the wife could be seen winnowing the rice or grinding spices such as fresh pepper or saffron between two stones. Cloves, nutmeg and mace had long been part of the cuisine of southern India, grew plentifully in the Caribbean and were quickly absorbed into the dishes of people who had come from quite different regions.

For the majority of Indians, life in the West Indies remained extremely basic until the middle of this century. They would always have ground whatever spices they could afford to buy themselves. Packaged curry powders, such as the much-loved 'Chefs', did not appear in the market place until some families had managed to make enough money to begin their own businesses and plastic made packaging a cheap and convenient possibility.

The Hindus who came to Trinidad brought with them their traditional vegetarian habits. Pumpkin, by now plentiful, was among their staple foods. It has always been cheap to buy and in the rainy season the vines grow all over any open ground, walls and ditches. Where people were very poor, they would nip off the side shoots and tips of the vine and make them into a curry. The fruit, which matures quickly and grows better in the islands than anywhere else, yields a rich warm yellow flesh. In Bengal it was traditional for the male member of the family to cut the pumpkin, since it represented a living sacrifice. This tradition has continued in the Caribbean, mystifying later generations of Indians who have retained the practice without remembering the reason for it. Today 'outside' or illegitimate children are called 'pumpkin vine children'.

You will never starve in the West Indies for people are always sharing their crops. I was given a pumpkin which kept for weeks before I could decide what to do with it. In the end I stuffed it with a goat curry, much enjoyed by Caribbean Indians. The original *kari*, anglicized to *curry*, originated in the south of India as a broth or soup to accompany a dish of rice. Where the peasant could afford it, he would have one curry with his rice and the wealthy several. This dish works on the same principle, with the pumpkin helping the curry to go a long way. If you live near a large Hindu community, you may be lucky enough to be able to find goat; otherwise use pork, for which I have written the recipe here.

 For **Pumpkin stuffed with Goat or Pork Curry** try to buy your pumpkin from a West Indian stall. The European variety do not have enough flavour. For four people choose a pumpkin weighing 1.5–2 kg (3–4 lbs), cut off the top where the stalk grows, and cut out the top of the pumpkin to approximately the size of a saucer. Scoop out the seeds and attached fibres. Put it in a pot large enough to hold it and fill with water three-quarters of the way up the side. Cover with a lid and bring

to the boil. It will take up to thirty minutes. Test with a knife, which should go in with just a little resistance, taking care not to pierce the outer skin. Put into a deep baking dish, fill with the curry and cook in a moderate oven for forty-five minutes. Careful judgment is needed not to overcook the pumpkin since you do not want the sides to collapse on the way to the table. For the curry filling you will need to marinade 1 kg (2 lbs) of pork, plus some extra bones, in 2 tablespoons of coconut oil, 1 tablespoon of wine vinegar, 1 teaspoon black pepper, 1 small finely chopped onion, 3 crushed cloves of garlic, 2 sprigs of fresh marjoram and ½ a teaspoon of freshly grated ginger. Rub well in and leave overnight. Remove all the seasoning and pat the meat dry. For the final cooking you will need 3–4 tablespoons of coconut oil, 30–60 g (1–2 oz) of white sugar, 600 ml (1 pint) of fresh coconut milk, 1 large finely chopped onion, 1 whole head of garlic cut in half horizontally, 2 tablespoons of curry powder, 1 teaspoon of black pepper, 1 teaspoon grated ginger, 1 hot pepper, ⅔ of the juice of a fresh lime and 1 teaspoon of salt. Heat the coconut oil and sugar until it is bubbling brown, then throw in the pork pieces and bones and fry until golden brown. Add all the onion, garlic, black pepper and curry powder, lower the heat and sweat the juices with a lid on. When the onion has melted away, add all the remaining ingredients except for the lime juice. Cook for 2 hours at a low tremble. You may find that the coconut oil appears to curdle or separate, but this will amalgamate later by itself. Remove the bones and the pepper, which should not have been allowed to burst. Then taste for salt and add the lime juice, stir well and put into the pumpkin. Place in a moderate oven for forty-five minutes. At the end of the cooking time you will find that the juices have penetrated the flesh of the pumpkin most deliciously. Any excess oil will have risen to the top and can be spooned off before serving.

Lobster was an ideal food that satisfied the standards of cleanliness, since they could buy it alive – packaged whole as it were – and it was not cut or cleaned until cooked.

For **Lobster Fruit Curry** for two, allow half a cooked lobster for each person. Cook it for no more than three minutes in water (ideally sea water but otherwise salted) that has been brought to the boil. Remove the flesh from the tail. Then very gently fry a hot pepper for three to four minutes in 200 ml (7¼ fl oz) of vegetable oil and 50 g (2 oz) unsalted butter, melted together. The pepper is only intended to flavour the oil; be sure to remove it after frying, or the flavours of this dish will be ruined. Then mince 1 large Spanish onion and fry in the same oil. When softened down, add 2 tablespoons of curry powder and ¼ teaspoon of freshly ground black pepper, waiting for them to heat through before stirring in, or the onions will seize. Cook gently for three to four minutes after mixing in, add 450 ml (15 fl oz) of fresh coconut milk and simmer for twenty minutes with the bones from the empty and cleaned lobster carapace. Take a ripe mango weighing about 250 g (8 oz), peel it and purée the flesh. In a pan heat a little coconut oil and fry 2 crushed cloves of garlic. Let them turn almost golden brown, giving off the hint of the slightest burn, then stir in the mango purée and a few drops of pepper sauce. Strain the coconut stock and add it to the mango purée. You could blend this but the contrast of textures is good. Add the lobster tails and warm through very slowly for five minutes.

Those Indians that came from the north of India were mostly Muslim. They brought with them food with strong Mogul and Persian influences; more subtle in its use of spices and herbs and sauces, and less hot than the south enjoyed. Mullet is marvellous in such a curry, with its muddy taste underlying that of the spices and curry leaves. Many Trinidad Indians have such a tree in their backyard. Its leaves are a greyish green and small and give off a curry-like scent.

For **Curried Mullet** allow 1 medium mullet per person and ask for it to be filleted. Have ready 1 medium finely chopped onion, 2 crushed cloves of garlic, 3–4 tablespoons of vegetable oil, ¼ teaspoon of mustard seeds, 4 cloves and 10 coriander seeds, fresh black pepper, a pinch of cayenne pepper, 1 tablespoon of curry powder, 600 ml (1 pint) of fish stock, 175 ml (6 fl oz) single cream, some rock salt to taste, a pinch of brown sugar and ¼ teaspoon of fresh lemon or lime juice. Fry the onion and garlic together until the garlic has a pleasant but slightly bitter taste, then add the mustard seeds. Stir in the cloves, coriander and black pepper, and fry for another three minutes. Add the fish stock, cayenne pepper, curry powder and salt, and simmer for five minutes. Pour in the cream and simmer carefully for a further five minutes, then lay in the fish fillets with a pinch of brown sugar. Turn off the heat and leave covered for half an hour, then add the lemon juice. Warm slightly to serve. Serve with boiled rice.

There was a shortage of women on the estates which began to have far-reaching effects into the traditional ways of Indian life. This often resulted in appalling violence towards the women and in some cases to murder. It became so widespread that the authorities became increasingly alarmed, and severe criticism of the system of indentureship followed. It would seem that as wave after wave of new arrivals of men from India came to the estates, they brought with them reminders to the established residents of old village links and customs. They were thus reinforced and perpetuated, inhibiting the Indian men from marrying women from any other race for fear of social chastisement when eventually they returned to India.

The women, on the other hand, often committed polyandry amongst their own kind as well as marrying into the other racial groups, causing ungovernable passion and wounded self-esteem amongst their menfolk. The reasons still remain unclear; perhaps the women were escaping from the awful drudgery of plantation life and by moving from one relationship to another hoped to improve their lot. Also, the women received their small wage in their own hands, giving them a new sense of independence.

The news of the women's apparent immorality eventually reached the Indian public, who were deeply offended, for they expected chastity in their womenfolk. According to Basdeo Mangru, who contributed to a group of essays to commemorate the 150th anniversary of their indentureship, 'their plight became the explosive feature of the indentureship system' and added power to the nationalist voice to have it brought to an end.

Death by hanging, the cat-o'-nine-tails and more careful vigilance did reduce the acts of barbarism by a dramatic fifty percent. But the scarcity of women continued and child-marriages became the norm. Charles Kingsley noted that, 'The girls are practically sold by their fathers while yet still children, often to wealthy men much older than they.'

Towards the end of indentureship the planters realized the importance of marital stability, especially since they wanted more labour without the cost of importing it, and so exercised their power to transfer a man, who was believed to be enticing another man's wife, to another estate.

Through the diary of Yseult Bridges, born in Trinidad in 1888, we learn of detailed aspects of the Indians' lives that on the whole were rarely recorded. The daughter of an unusual island marriage which brought together a French aristocratic family and the English plantocracy, her account beautifully illustrates a world that was not to last very much longer. She wrote of the tenants on the estates: 'My mother took a great interest in them . . . they lived in whitewashed thatched houses made of mud and thatch, set amongst plots of land from which they earned their livelihood.' At Christmas time her mother gave a party for them under the cocoa house, distributing presents from the Christmas tree. Cones of sugar loaves called *papelons*, which were traditionally covered in tightly wrapped layers of banana leaves tied at the top and then trimmed into a rosette, were given to any expectant mother. Yseult wrote of these gifts: 'How dark and rich and succulent they were. And how delicious spread over butter on those crisp little loaves of bread which the baker delivered each morning.' To the outsider it may appear very thoughtful, but giving sugar to those same workers who cut the cane seems extraordinarily insensitive.

Yseult also gives us a good insight into the preparations for a traditional wedding. Her father contributed a goat in kid and her mother a hen with a brood of chickens to the family, as was customary. The grandparents asked the estate owner for permission to build a hut for the couple, who would then live by cultivating the land. The labourers from the surrounding fields came to help construct the simple dwelling. In India they used mud bricks plastered with adobe; here they collected tapia grass and bamboo strips as a frame for the mud walls which, once dry, had an astonishing resilience.

Naipaul wrote of the same custom in the 1960s. 'For three days they laboured with all hands from the fields to erect a bamboo frame and coconut branches for a roof. The bamboo had to be specially cut and carried in from the cool glades and ravines where it grew.' The roof was then thatched. At home they used reeds; here they adopted the palm. The earth floor was beaten flat and in the days to come, as the earth disintegrated, the chickens would come in to take a dust bath and escape from the sweltering heat of the day outside. People today still remember the chore of having to constantly sweep and flatten the floor.

At the back of the house, a derelict looking structure was erected to function as the kitchen. Often the trimmed branches of trees were used for the supports and roofs; then anything that could be was scrounged to infill the walls, from tin, bamboo and shop boxes. The wood-smoke from the fires under the coal pots soon blackened the different textures and surfaces, until the whole room adopted a perpetual darkened cohesive look by day and by night. A description of such a lean-to kitchen by an English colonel, Kenny-Herbert, who was in India in the second half of the nineteenth century, suggests that the formula varied little from those built back home. He wrote: 'The kitchen was no part of the house proper . . . the room is constructed with as little ventilation and light as possible.' He went on to say that there was no scullery, no place for washing up – hence a 'noisome cesspool' outside – and no chimney to remove smoke or fumes, which instead coated the inside of the shed with ancient layers of soot. 'The floor is of mother earth, greasy black and cruelly uneven.' He ended by saying that it was not an exaggeration to state that not one in twenty Indian kitchens possessed proper equipment; 'The batterie de cuisine of people with two thousand rupees a month, and more is frequently inferior to that of a humble cottager in Britain.' I have talked with Indians in the Caribbean today who recall, almost with nostalgia, how they often helped their grandparents clean such kitchens, beating the earthen floors flat again, to be ready for any special occasion; and who also remember the hectic preparations for weddings. The food would be cooked over an open fire-hole in the yard. Great fire-blackened cauldrons were begged or borrowed from the estate kitchens or wealthier relatives. All through the night the women stayed up peeling potatoes, cleaning rice, slicing and cutting vegetables to the accompaniment of singing. Enormous quantities of food were needed to feed all the members of family who would gather for the wedding. It was commonplace to slaughter goats, which would have begun at dawn.

A shoulder of lamb weighing 1.5–2 kg (3–4 lbs) substitutes well for goat, should you fail to find it, in this recipe for **Caribbean Curried Goat** for four to six people. Cut the meat into cubes for marinading. Finely chop 1½ onions and crush 1 clove of garlic. Mix these with 2 teaspoons of wine vinegar, 3 teaspoons fresh lemon juice and some salt. Rub all this into the meat. Fry the meat and bones in oil and sugar until it turns a good rich golden brown, then add 1 large minced Spanish onion, 3 cloves of crushed garlic and some salt. Lower to a moderate heat, cover with the lid and let the juices sweat out for twenty minutes or so. Add approximately 3 cm (1 inch) of freshly grated ginger, 1–2 tablespoons of curry powder. Dissolve a vegetable stock cube into 450 ml (¾ pint) of boiling water and add to the pot. Stir well and be prepared to simmer for at least two hours on a low heat. Remove the meat and bone to serve. If the stock is too thin, reduce with some fast boiling. Do not add any thickening agents; it will ruin the taste. Return the meat to the sauce to heat through before serving. The spices preserved the dish through the heat of the day until the evening festivities. In fact the dish improved in flavour.

Hindu couples underwent separate wedding ceremonies. At the bridegroom's house the celebrations lasted for a week. On the last evening, wrote Yseult, 'It was a lovely, still starlit night, and a great concourse of East Indians gathered in a circle.' In the centre sat the bridegroom, surrounded by a ring of lights that flickered, catching the oiled polish on his skin. Clad only in a loin-cloth, he was crowned with tinsel interwoven with pink frangipani blossoms which fell around his shoulders. All the flowers for weddings were supplied by the Indian market gardeners. This seems to have been their speciality. While the bridegroom sat motionless, drums were beaten, priests chanted and dancers in traditional dress wound their bodies with sinewed control, the bells on their ankles seduced into a sympathetic musical life of their own.

Brass platters were brought out, piled high with the rice, sacrificial meats, sauces and a variety of pickles to accompany them. Since certain fruits were extremely cheap, often there for the picking, it would have cost almost nothing to have pickles and sauces made from them to accompany the main dishes. The following pickles make excellent accompaniments.

The Indians make much use of the fruit of the tamarind tree. It originally grew wild in tropical Africa, but was taken to India and then later to the West Indies. It produces a prolific number of tawny-brown pods, which hold the slimy, tart, dark-brown pulp which can be eaten fresh. In the West Indies they use it in curries, preserves, sauces and chutneys. The wood was invaluable for making really good and much valued charcoal.

You can now buy the tamarind seeds in packets to make **Tamarind Sauce**. If you buy them loose, you need to take off the brittle outer shell. Weigh 100–125 g (4 oz) of tamarind seeds into 350 ml (12 fl oz) of boiling water. Leave to cool. Use some of this water to help push the pulp that surrounds the seeds through a sieve with a spoon, leaving behind the seeds. Put into a pan the prepared tamarind paste, 15 mm (½ inch) of fresh ginger – grated, 50 g (2 oz) of demerara sugar, a pinch of cayenne or a drop of pepper sauce and a little salt to taste. Mix them together and simmer for fifteen minutes, stirring occasionally. This is a marvellous accompaniment to game.

In Grenada we pick green mangos locally to make Caribbean-Indian pickle. It is named after the old Westerhall estate we live on. For **Westerhall Pickle** grate a green mango which is a quarter of its way to being ripe (these subtleties take a lifetime to learn, but it does not matter if you are slightly out). Peel and grate it along with half a small onion. Add the juice of a fresh lime and ¼ teaspoon of salt, a teaspoon of cider vinegar, a few drops of pepper sauce and mix all this together with 1 tablespoon of good olive oil.

Unlike the previous pickles which are made from raw ingredients, this one will need to be cooked.

 For **Melongene Pickle** you will need 1 kg (2 lbs) of aubergine, 60 g (2 oz) each of garlic and freshly peeled ginger, 250 g (8 oz) of demerara sugar, 250 ml (8 fl oz) of cider vinegar, 50 ml (4 fl oz) oil, chilli peppers to taste, 4 cloves, a teaspoon each of coriander seeds, turmeric and curry powder, and lastly a pinch of *jeera*. Chop very finely the garlic and ginger. Mix the vinegar and sugar to dissolve and set aside. In a heavy pan heat the oil and fry the *jeera*, coriander, cloves, chilli, turmeric and curry powder gently for three minutes. Add the garlic and ginger and fry for another minute. Stir in the sugar and vinegar, frying for a further minute or two, add the bringal, mix together well and cook the pickle for ten to fifteen minutes at a simmer.

Late in the evening, brass platters would have followed with sweet cakes such as *jilebi*, *ladoo*, *maleeda* or a sweet made from tamarind seeds. To Western tastebuds these small dumplings are a confusion of tastes; salt, sweet and sour from the tamarind fruit.

A blessing for the couple's house was always desirable, usually following close on the heels of a wedding. Further ceremonies were then enacted. The holy man who was to be the pundit that day would arrive carrying his pundit's garb in a cardboard suitcase.

While indentureship continued, life continued on the estates unchanged; the old men would gather to talk, drink their rum and smoke. Many still could not speak English and were not interested in their new island life. Talk was invariably of returning home to India one day, although, as Naipaul wrote, 'when the opportunity came many refused, afraid of the unknown, afraid to leave the familiar temporariness.' Instead their conversation, gently rising and falling with the night, invoked memories of the world they had lost: a muslin *dupatta* wrapped around a woman's head; night scents of lavender and *chambele*; men in red *dhotis* fishing on lakes whose frozen waters were fed from the Himalayas; farmers whose faces had been sculpted by the winds into brown rippling hide; camphor burners; the consecrated nectar of the prayer room.

They brought with them a prodigious store of epics, fables and folk wisdom, such as the Puranas, which were ancient books in Sanskrit concerned with historical and legendary matters. 'The philosophy of our coolies in this colony', wrote J. H. Collins in Trinidad, 'is substantially that which their forefathers adopted some 2,500 years ago . . . it must be acknowledged that the Puranas are a mass of contradictions, extravagance and idolatry couched in highly poetical language.'

The planters and visiting officials never took the trouble to grasp or understand the language or culture of the Indian. Collins showed this when he saw the Indians chanting their Hindu prayers or field songs, mistaking them for the Puranas. He continued that it was 'astonishing how familiar the Trinidad coolies are with them, even down to the humble labourers who till our fields . . . you may often see them crouching down in a semi-circle chanting whole stanzas of the epic poems'. The men still wore scarves in the traditional way, wrapped around their heads; only the dull red glow of the clay *cheelum* would identify their squatting circles.

The conversation and recitals would run on through the night, the perfumes of the night blossoms released as intermittently as the aroma of the puffs of *ganja*. The Hindus, who revered the Indian hemp as a holy plant, brought the first seed to the islands. It was the sugar planters who soon determined that while the Indian found comfort from the reality of his appalling life by smoking, he nevertheless did less work on it, and so pushed through legislation against it. However, its values were quickly recognized by other groups such as the Africans, who adopted its uses as a tonic against the flu by making a tea, or steeping it with rum or wine, with or without pimento seeds. Others incorporated it into their pastries, or used it as a vegetable. Under its Spanish name, *sensemilla*, *ganja* has become part of West Indian culture, but the planters were never as open about using it as the others were. As an alternative relaxation at these nocturnal gatherings, the Indians turned to rum – White Cock, Indian Maiden or Parakeet. Whatever their choice, it oiled memory's wheels.

The evening conversations, the weddings and other religious festivities were brief respites between the sameness of long working days as hard as those of the Portuguese or African in earlier centuries. The West Indian planters remained as committed as ever to the lucrative cultivation of sugar. As Charles Kingsley commented on his return from the islands in 1874, 'What will be the future of agriculture in the West Indies . . . the profits from sugar growing, despite all the drawbacks, have of late been very great.' And so the hard labour on the plantations continued, the pace accelerated by the introduction of trains linking San Fernando to Port of Spain. Estates near the new line went up in value. In the great houses the old-fashioned luxury of the planters' lifestyle continued much as it had done in the previous century. 'Here, in the beautiful old homes, the traditional life of the West Indies still lingers and the hospitality prevails as of yore,' wrote a member of one plantation-owning family in Trinidad about the turn of the century.

Guests arrived from miles around for the celebration of the cane harvest 'crop-over', riding in splendour in their carriages with their gala attire carried in panniers strapped to mules ridden by their attendants. Immense tessellated verandahs with deep lounge chairs invited ease, while the retainers who had spent a lifetime in the service of the family carried around immense Sheffield-plate salvers weighed down with tumblers of Planters Punch. At dinner an almost eighteenth-century elegance reigned. Afterwards they waltzed through the warm night to the music of Johann Strauss.

Many of the estates were still owned by a close-knit French aristocratic elite descended from royalist immigrants who had come to the island just before the French Revolution. These fifty families followed lives steeped in tradition and self-esteem. Yseult Bridges described how at four every afternoon the servants would arrange her mother, with a rustling of silk petticoats and billowing gauzy skirts, on the verandah to receive visitors. 'She greeted them in exactly the manner she deemed the circumstance required. Her smile was always in evidence, but its quality, the angle of her handshake and the whole poise of her body were nicely adjusted to correspond with the social distinction of the visitors.'

Marriage outside the closely interrelated group was unthinkable, even until fairly recent times. In one of Evelyn Waugh's novels, a French Creole girl returning home to Trinidad from Paris explains to the hero that she is not yet engaged. 'But you see, there are so few young men I can marry. They must be Catholic and of an island family.' More than that, they needed birth and breeding. As one of the de Verteuilles family wrote in 1932, with reference to other planter families, 'I still have that which they cannot buy.' Of course non-legal unions with all other groups abounded.

And so the plantation system continued, as if frozen in time, well into this century. The vast number of Indians remained tied to the estates, unable to improve their low standard of living. Indentureship continued and was only interrupted by the outbreak of the First World War. The Indian National Congress worked hard towards greater self-government for the Indian people, and constantly pressured the Government. However, it was not until 1916 that the Government legislated that it should come to an end within five years. Some began to own their own land, helped by planters who gave them small parcels of land to avoid having to keep their promise of paying repatriation expenses.

Of their cultivating habits it was noted at the time that the Indian engaged in market gardening practised a very strict economy; nothing was wasted. Each type of vegetable, from cabbage, lettuce, callaloo and garden eggs, had its own bed which was better tended than the African's, who preferred a wilderness of mingled products. They sold their garden produce to the Chinese shopkeepers or joined the established parade of African and Chinese *marchands* to the back verandah. By now they used donkey-drawn carts to carry their produce, specializing in the sale of charcoal for kitchen braziers and green coconuts, the sweet and nutty waters of which were then thought to be a fine tonic for the kidneys.

Moving back and forth in the luxuriously green fields, the buffalo laboured under the wooden yoke resting on their necks, their skin rubbed raw until they developed sores and skin cancer, their life expectancy only three to ten years. Committed to one view only, yoked between the shafts, trekking from the cane fields to the train and hauling intolerable loads of cut canes, it was said that they would not pull the carts unless they could hear the creaking of the carriage wheels as encouragement. At the refineries the furnaces roared night and day throughout the season, the workers collecting the sackfuls of sugar brought from the train, to keep up the supply for the enormous copper vats of crushed cane juices.

The Indians also became the 'crabmen' and took over the oyster trade from the Chinese. They have held it to this day. Drive around the Savannah in the Port of Spain, not so long ago a sugar estate, and you will find the oyster trade still flourishing. The extraordinary architectural style of the buildings describes Trinidad's recent history. Seven magnificent mansions – built by eighteenth-century grandees – ranging from German and Scottish baronial style to French Baroque colonial, dominate two sides of the old tropical gardens shaded by giant trees. Here the bell-like blossoms of the jacaranda cast their gentle violet light into the heated air. At night the park lights are brilliant, each ringed with a shimmering humid haze under a star-studded indigo evening sky. Here you can watch the traditional skills of the Indian oysterman working at his oyster stall, which as Naipaul described, 'was yellowly, smokily lit by a flambeau with a thick spongy wick'. The oysters lie faceted, grey and black, in shining heaps. Next to them are bottles containing red and yellow pepper-sauce, each of which is stoppered with a twist of brown paper. There is always great activity surrounding the cleaning and washing of them. Short blunt knives deftly flick the cleaned shells and then they are washed again. As the pepper-sauce goes into each oyster, it is swallowed straight down, the raw flesh smell of the oyster heightening its flavour.

Today the majority of East Indians in the Caribbean, still Hindu, live in rural communities from farming. Some did manage by the end of the nineteenth century to do well enough for themselves through hard thrift and industry. They divorced themselves from the estates and educated their children to other professions. By 1921 there were virtually no Indians still resident on the estates, but in the villages they managed to keep a more traditional and cultural way of life, albeit in an adapted form, until the 1950s when education for boys and girls brought great changes.

Many still live in very large family groups, one generation upon another, as so well written about by Naipaul. Their homes are distinguishable by the array of old and new flags raised beside the house, fluttering forlornly in the trade winds.

The darkest night of September is always chosen to celebrate the festival of Diwali to honour Lakshimi, the goddess of light, riches and loveliness. Men from the villages cut the bamboo to make the supports for the handmade *deyas*, clay pots filled with coconut oil to feed the lighted wick. On such nights they have no need to light their hurricane lamps, for the lights are placed thick on the ground, covering paths, roads, culverts, parapets and bridges. The children run from lamp to lamp, changing the wicks to keep them burning and so prolong the night.

Janice Shinebourne, the Guyanese writer, recently wrote in her novel, *The Last English Plantation*, that by choosing the darkest night they would feel the symbolism of the lights more intensely and 'the meaning of exile and return deepened'. She tells of the legends surrounding it, of Indian empires and the myths of Indian kings, queens, princesses and princes; 'the movement of royal deities between the celestial and earthly, between exile and return . . . the myth absorbed the humiliation of their plantation existence.'

Food is the tradition of gift, especially a sacrificial dish called *parsad* which is made of sugar, milk and raisins mixed with flour into a dough and cooked. Then, around the full moon in March, Phagwa is celebrated with much dancing in carnival spirit. A more subdued celebration is Eid-ul Fitr on the new moon of Ramadan. Traditional dress is worn and families visit each other, holding magnificent dinners to which they invite their friends from other ethnic groups.

Today the choice of dishes on the menu of each festival is interchangeable, although there are certain dishes that are still traditional. For Eid, you will be offered dishes such as curried goat, *dahl*, *paratha* or *sewain*, a rich concoction of fine vermicelli, sugar, almonds and evaporated milk.

A much respected Trinidad writer on food, Sylvia Hunt included the following recipe for *sewain* in her book of recipes representing all the different races who had come to live in the region.

To prepare **Sewain** for eight people you will need 1 kg (2 lbs) of fine vermicelli broken into small pieces and fried in 25 g (1 oz) of *ghee*, until it has turned a golden toasted brown. Have ready a pot with 1 litre (1¾ pints) of boiling water and put in the vermicelli, 2 tablespoons of white sugar, 2 cinnamon sticks and 3 pods of cardamon skin with its seeds crushed. Boil this for fifteen minutes, she says, until the vermicelli is 'swollen and slippery' then add 1½ cans of evaporated milk and ½–1 can of condensed milk, a teaspoon of almond essence and a handful of slivered almonds. This can be presented hot or cold. It is a fairly sweet and heavy dish, so small portions would be enough.

Another of the festival dishes, this time for Diwali, is to my mind one of the most distinctive of all Caribbean–Indian recipes. A *chataigne* curry is served alongside curried chickpeas and potatoes or curried mango.

The use of breadnut or *chataigne* in a curry today bears out what Naipaul meant when he wrote, 'We were steadily adopting the food styles of others: the Portuguese stew of tomatoes, in which anything might be done. The Negro way with yams, plantains and breadfruit. Everything we adopted became our own and so it was with the breadnut.'

The breadnut, sometimes called *chataigne*, is not to be confused with the breadfruit. They do look very alike, both being the same large greenish fruit, but the former bears seeds inside that taste very like our chestnut, while the other does not. Their origins are Polynesian and the fruits are distinguished easily enough by their outer skin, which in the case of the breadnut is prickly and the breadfruit smooth and hexagonally marked, rather like snake skin.

Both the pulp surrounding the seeds and the seeds themselves are curried by the Indian population as well as others today. They peel off the skin and cut the flesh into small pieces. The seeds are then peeled also. Then they fry the onion and freshly ground curry spices, before adding the chopped breadnut and seeds. Once the pieces have been tossed to coat them thoroughly with the oil and spices, they are left to simmer until soft, covered with fresh coconut milk. Sometimes saltfish or shrimps are added which is a delicious addition.

The fruit of the breadnut is curried when still green; when the skin has turned brown, only the seeds are used. These I detach from the protective fruit around them and wash, then boil them in their skins just as you would chestnuts until they are soft. After peeling them I usually simply chop them up and drop them into a meat curry twenty minutes before the meat has finished cooking.

And so the festivals continue, but each successive generation becomes more distant from the last. Memories and customs of Naipaul's childhood were sometimes mysterious. He wrote, 'Increasingly I understand that my Indian memories, the memories of that India which lived on into my childhood in Trinidad are like trapdoors into a bottomless past.'

THE TROPICAL UMBRELLA

*The Caribbean was bourne like an elliptical basin
in the hands of acolytes, and a people were absolved
of a history they did not commit.*

Derek Walcott

By the outbreak of the Second World War, nowhere could you find a stronger reflection of English society than in the islands of the Caribbean. But the war fanned a flame that had long been dormant, new hopes were kindled and the local people's ambitions were echoed in the song that ran, 'I going to plant fight for a thousand years', sung by the Trinidadian who called himself Growling Tiger. The singer did not anticipate Churchill leasing off parts of the Caribbean islands to the Americans and the focus shifting forever from Europe to the United States.

Today it is Trinidad that has the largest number of each cultural group still living there. By 1970 the figures for the different immigrant groups showed that the Africans formed the largest section, of roughly 400,000, followed closely in number by the East Indians. There were marginally fewer Chinese than Europeans, who totalled around 11,000. The Portuguese seemed to have disappeared altogether (but are to be found as a substantial group in Guyana), and twenty-six Amerindians appeared to have survived until the late 1940s.

Amerindian artifacts and words such as barbecue, tobacco, hammock, canoe and hurricane, are at the moment our only reminder of their existence, although recently serious archaeological work is being done in the islands to learn more about the Amerindian. William Keegan, an anthropologist of the Florida Museum of Natural History, wrote: 'Interpretations of West Indian pre-history exhibit a strong reliance on contact-period reports.' These were the records and writings of Columbus, Las Casas and Oviedo amongst others, who were there at the opening up of the New World. 'They were often', he continued, 'used in the absence of archaeological corroboration.'

The remainder of the groups have all left infinitely more. They once called as vendors at the back door of the great house, but now they sell their produce in the market-place and everyone else goes to buy from them. Every ingredient needed to supply the variety of different dishes can now be found here, and one of the most integrated markets is to be found in the Port of Spain. Often the markets are housed in old open-sided colonial buildings decorated with rusting Victorian ironwork. The galvanized roofs penetrate an intolerable heat down on the vendors, almost as strong as the sun outside. Some of them take advantage of the shade that the market building affords and have moved inside, displaying their goods on raised stalls. There are bundles, baskets and jars of every imaginable spice for sale.

It is here, in the market-place, that you may see the beginning and end of processes. One has bought and used cinnamon, for example, but where did it come from, how does it grow and what does it really look like? In the Caribbean the broad sheets of rich-red bark are sold cut and rolled into cigar lengths. Chew one and there is a heat and sweetness you would not suspect. A local person will feel pride in showing you it growing under hazy-blue skies in the damp early morning, with the dew rising and the birds exulting. The green leaves of the cinnamon tree shadow the ground where the bark has been stripped and laid, the freshly torn tree pours its heady oiled scent into the still tropical air as strip after strip is taken and left to dry. There are so many processes we take for granted. Strange as it may seem, I feel more whole for seeing the beginning and end of this product.

Many of the market women still prefer to sit out under the blazing sun with their produce spread in front of them on the ground, as they have always done. Their fruit has all been grown in distant garden parishes. The display is such that only Gauguin could have captured it: giant pineapples, papaya at varying stages of ripeness from green to yellow, exotic naseberries, blushy red Ethiopian apples, garlands of 'ortanique' oranges and tangerines, piles of unwieldy looking root vegetables, red and purple sweet potatoes, enormous brown hairy yams and many hands of green bananas. Live crabs, their legs tied with a local vine, lie alongside the leaves of the freshly picked and prized callaloo. Chickens stand on one leg until they are sold and carried away, the hapless creatures tucked unprotesting under their buyers' arms.

Listen to the African woman buying her ground provisions. She is using the language first taken there from England. Shakespeare in *As You Like It* gave his character Jacques instructions for the hunters, 'shoot the deer and kill them up'. She explains that her shopping is for 'a cook up', which they will 'nyam' or eat and enjoy. This word has spread right around the Caribbean basin. She is also expert in choosing the freshest of the yams, eddoes and sweet potatoes, where I can see no difference. She will advise you if you feel unwell; green papaya will reduce hypertension, mashed green banana will cure stomach ulcers.

Although the statistics only allow that the Portuguese have survived in any numbers in Guyana, there are nevertheless a hundred or so more in Barbados, and without doubt a few still live in Trinidad and Grenada. Like the others who came before and after them, they gradually abandoned their language and their culture began to wane also. Wealthy Portuguese managed to return to Madeira to renew old ties, but sent their children to England to be educated. Nonetheless, their salt-cod, garlic pork, olive oil and wine are in evidence everywhere in the southern Caribbean.

It was under the same roof that I met Mrs Chung-Steele of the Bird's Nest Restaurant; her menus are now very sophisticated. She is buying live chickens to make the stock for bird's nest soup, which would have been unthinkable a few years ago, and the swiftlet nests are flown in from the Far East via New York. The Chinese prize the taste so much that for generations men have risked their lives to climb hundreds of feet up on precarious bamboo structures to collect the nests from the caves. Now the Chinese in the Caribbean can afford to import them. This is how much their lives have changed. She went on to tell me how she returned to China with her father in the 1960s to trace their family. They took with them the seeds of the tomato plant and carrots, which were enormously appreciated there, but her family were unprepared for the shock of not being understood, for the particular dialect had been overrun by Mandarin.

The same market now provides all the intricate spices the Indian needs and can now afford for his curries, such as *hardi, menthi* seeds, *jeera* – prepared to an exact burnt flavour – vegetables such as *caraille* with its bitter sweet flavour and okras and *bajhi*. Cutting the grass from the top of the cane every evening to feed the animals, the Indian still speaks of the blades of grass as 'cane meat', unaware that he has adopted the old English usage of meat, meaning food in general. Today, the old men may still talk of India as home, but few return there. 'It isn't my home and cannot be my home,' wrote Naipaul after a visit to India, 'I am at once too far and too close.'

Usually the fish market is close to the sea; again all the groups will buy the same fish though they may prepare it rather differently. Here a real heat is built up not just from the sun's rays, but from the women's fiendish application in hacking the great fish such as the tuna and shark apart. You do not argue, but accept whatever the stroke of the machete has severed from the body of the fish lying stiffly, the skin shimmering and the gashes in the thick flesh pouring brilliant red blood over the chipped white tiles. Outside in the gutter, more women sit selling much smaller fish such as jacks and the odd live crab. The range is slowly diminishing as more and more of it is exported to the French islands, America and Europe.

Step across the road to the sea wall and you will feel the trade winds embrace you, cool and fresh from their path across five thousand miles of Atlantic waters. It was these trade winds that blew the discoverers and builders to the New World from Europe five hundred years ago. Nowadays one can span these worlds in a day. I no longer feel that I am leaving one for another, for they are inextricably linked by a past that is shared.

BIBLIOGRAPHY

ATKINS, JOHN *A Voyage to Guinea, Brazil and the West Indies in HMS Swallow and Weymouth: with Remarks on the Gold, Ivory and Slave Trade*, 1735; Frank Cass, London 1970

BECKWITH, M. *Black Roadways: A Study in Jamaican Folk Life*, Chapel Hill, 1929

BEHN, APHRA *Oroonoko*, 1688; Methuen, London 1986

BRERETON, BRIDGET *A History of Modern Trinidad 1783–1962*, Heinemann Educational, London 1981

BRIDGES, YSEULT *A Child in the Tropics*, Aquarela Galleries, Trinidad and Tobago 1988

CALALOUX, MAHABIR NOOR KUMAR *Tobago During Indentureship 1845–1917*, Tacarigua, Trinidad 1985

CAMPBELL, A. A. *St Thomas Negros*, vol IV no. 5, 1943

CANOT, THEODORE *Adventures of an African Slaver*, 1854; M. Cowley (Ed.), London 1928

CARMICHAEL, GERTRUDE *The History of the West Indian Island of Trinidad*, London 1961

CARMICHAEL, A. C. *Domestic Manners and Social Conditions of the White, Coloured and Negro Populations of the West Indies*, 1833; facsimile edition, Greenwood Press, London

COLERIDGE, H. N. *Six Months in Trinidad in 1825*, 1825; facsimile edition, Greenwood Press, London

COLT, SIR HENRY from *Colonising Expedition to the West Indies & Guiana*, London 1925

DABYDEEN, DR DAVID & SAMAROO, BRINSLEY (Eds) *India in the Caribbean*, Hansib Publishing, London 1987

DARK, P. J. *Bush Negro Art*, Alec Tiranti, London 1954

DAVID, ELIZABETH *English Bread and Yeast Cookery*, Penguin, London 1970

DAVID, ELIZABETH *Spices, Salts and Aromatics in the English Kitchen*, Allen Lane, London 1977

DAVIDSON, BASIL *Africa in History*, 1968; Paladin, London 1975

DAVIDSON, BASIL *Africa: History of a Continent*, Hamlyn, London 1970

DAVIDSON, BASIL *A History of West Africa 1000–1800*, Longman, London 1977

Details from the letters of Bishop Etheridge in Essequibo to Father Provincial in London 1857–1869, Jesuit Archive, London

DOOKHAM, ISAAC *A Post-Emancipation History of the West Indies*, Longman Caribbean, Trinidad 1981

DUDLEY, SIR ROBERT *The Voyage of Sir Robert Dudley*, London 1793

ENCISO, N. FERNANDEZ *A Brief Summary of Geographie*, Seville 1519; translated from Spanish by Roger Barlow, Hakluyt Society, 1932

FERDINAND, SIR EVERARD *Among the Indians of Guiana*, 1883; Dover Classics, London 1967

FREYRE, GILBERTO *Masters and Slaves*, New York 1946

FROUDE, JAMES ANTHONY *The English in the West Indies*, 1969

GATES, HENRY LOUIS (Ed.) *The Classic Slave Narrative*, 'The Interesting Life of Olaudah Equiano' [known as Gustavus Vassa], 1789; Mentor, New York 1987

GOSSE, HENRY *A Naturalistic Sojourn in Jamaica*, Longman, London 1851

HALL, DOUGLAS *In Miserable Slavery*, Macmillan Caribbean, 1989

HERSKOVITS, M. J. *An Ancient West African Kingdom*, 2 vols, New York 1938

HERSKOVITS, M. J. *The Myth of the Negro Past*, New York 1941

HERSKOVITS, M. J. & F. S. *A Trinidad Village*, Alfred Knopf, New York 1947

HUNT, SYLVIA *Menus for Festivals*, Bank of Commerce Trust Co., Trinidad and Tobago 1989

HUXLEY, ALDOUS *Beyond the Mexique Bay*, Penguin, London 1934

JOHNSON, HOWARD (Ed.) *After the Crossing: Minorities in a Creole Society*, Frank Cass, London 1988

JOSEPH, E. L. (Ed.) *History of Trinidad*, 1838; Frank Cass, London 1970

KINGSLEY, CHARLES *At Last a Christmas in the West Indies*, New York, 1851

KOPYTOFF, BARBARA from *The Anthropologist's Cookbook*, Jessica Kuper (Ed.), Routledge & Kegan Paul, London 1979

LANCASTER, SIR JAMES *The Voyages of Sir James Lancaster*, Hakluyt Society, 1877

LEVY, JAQUELINE 'Chinese Indentured Immigration to Jamaica in the Latter Part of the 19th Century', paper presented in 1972 to the Conference of Caribbean Historians

LEWICKI, TADEUSZ *West African Food in the Middle Ages, According to Arabic Sources*, Cambridge University Press, Cambridge 1974

LEWIS, MATTHEW *Journal of a West Indian Proprietor: Kept During a Residence in the Island of Jamaica*, 1834; Greenwood Press, London 1929

LIGON, RICHARD *A True and Exact History of the Island of Barbados*, 1657; Frank Cass, London 1970

LONG, EDWARD *The History of Jamaica*, 3 vols. 1774; Frank Cass, London 1970

MACCULLUM, PIERRE *A Political Account of the Island of Trinidad*, Liverpool 1805

MORETON, J. B. *West Indian Manners & Customs*, London 1793

MORYSON, FYNES *An Itinerary Written by Fynes Moryson*, Gent, London 1617

MOUNTAIN, DIDYMUS *The Gardener's Labyrinth*, London

NAIPAUL, V. S. *An Area of Darkness*, Penguin, London 1964

NAIPAUL, V. S. *The Loss of El Dorado*, Penguin, London 1969

NAIPAUL, V. S. *A Wounded Civilization*, Penguin, London 1977

NEWTON, A. P. *European Nations in the West Indies 1493–1688*, A. & C. Black, London 1933

NUTTALL, GEOFFREY (Ed.) *Letters of John Pinney 1679–1699*, Oxford University Press, Oxford 1939

OLDMIXON, JOHN *The British Empire in America*, 1741; Kelley Publishers, 1970

OLSEN, FRED *On the Trail of the Arawaks*, University of Oklahoma, Oklahoma 1974

PARES, RICHARD *A West India Fortune*, London 1950

PRICE, N. *Behind the Planters Back*, Macmillan Caribbean, 1988

PURSEGLOVE, JOHN W. *Tropical Crops*, Longman, London 1968

RALEIGH, SIR WALTER *Discovery of Guiana*, (Sir R. Schomburgk Ed.) Hakluyt Society, 1848

RATTRAY, R. S. *Religion and Art in Ashanti*, Oxford 1927

ROUSE, IRVING *The Caribbean Area*, University of Chicago Press

SHINEBOURNE, JANICE *The Last English Plantation*, Peepal Tree Press, Leeds 1988

'Spring Plantation Papers 1744–1800', from the Ashton Court Collection, Bristol Archives

SPRINGER, RITA *Caribbean Cookbook*, Evans Bros, London 1969

TANNAHILL, REAY *Food in History*, Penguin, London 1973

TROLLOPE, ANTHONY *The West Indies and the Spanish Main*, London 1859

WALCOTT, DEREK *The Star Apple Kingdom*, Jonathan Cape, London 1980

WIGFIELD, WALTER MACDONALD *The Monmouth Rebels*, Alan Sutton, Gloucester 1985

WILLIAMS, DE ERIC *History of the People of Trinidad and Tobago*, Andre Deutsch, London 1964

WOLFE, LINDA *The Cooking of the Caribbean Islands*, Time Life Books, London 1970

INDEX OF RECIPES

GENERAL INDEX